Geometric Period *Plithos* Burial Ground at *Chora* of Naxos Island, Greece: Anthropology Report

Anagnostis P. Agelarakis

ARCHAEOPRESS PUBLISHING LTD
Gordon House
276 Banbury Road
Oxford OX2 7ED

www.archaeopress.com

ISBN 978 1 78491 303 8
ISBN 978 1 78491 304 5 (e-Pdf)

© Archaeopress and A P Agelarakis 2016

All rights reserved. No part of this book may be reproduced or transmitted,
in any form or by any means, electronic, mechanical, photocopying or otherwise,
without the prior written permission of the copyright owners.

Contents

Prologue 1

Geometric Component Burial Contexts and Anthropological Remains 2

Anatomic Distribution of Preserved Skeletal Remains 3

Aspects of Population Sample Demographic Profile 4

    Biological Sex Assessments 4

    Age Assessments 5

On Skeletal Morphology 7

Palaeopathological Profile 11

    Palaeopathologic Conditions 11

    Trauma Manifestations 14

Non-Anthropological Organic Materials of Burial Contexts with Emphasis on Faunal Remains 16

Epilogue 19

References Cited 21

Acknowledgements 23

Graphs 24

Tables 53

List of Graphs and Tables

Graph 1	25
Graph 2	25
Graph 3	26
Graph 4	27
Graph 5	28
Graph 6	29
Graph 7	30
Graph 8	30
Graph 9	31
Graph 10	32
Graph 11	32
Graph 12	33
Graph 13	33
Graph 14	34
Graph 15	34
Graph 16	35
Graph 17	36
Graph 18	37
Graph 19	37
Graph 20	38
Graph 20a	38
Graph 21	39
Graph 21a	39
Graph 22	40
Graph 22a	40
Graph 23	41
Graph 23a	41
Graph 24	42
Graph 25	43
Graph 26	43
Graph 27	44
Graph 28	44

Graph 29 45
Graph 30 45
Graph 31 46
Graph 32 47
Graph 33 48
Graph 34 48
Graph 35 49
Graph 36 50
Graph 37 51
Graph 38 51
Graph 39 52
Graph 40 52

Table 1 54
Table 2 86
Table 3 86
Table 4 86
Table 5 87

Prologue

Significant questions remain unanswered regarding the dynamics of the human condition that prevailed during the transitional period within the Early Iron Age, from the ProtoGeometric into the Geometric Period in ancient Greece. Sustained population growth in mainland and island communities in augmenting demographic stability, economic growth and incentives for long distance trade, support for the resurgence of the letters and arts, developments in the domains of the political milieu and administrative organizational abilities, as well as the availability of necessary diplomatic and military capacities must have been some of the critical objectives, decisive prerequisites, for the emerging contexts and subsequent sovereignty of the early city-states (Ahlberg 1971; Boardman 1998; Coldstream 2003; Hesiod; Kirk 1949; Kourou 1984; 1998; and 1999; Lambrinoudakis 1988; Moore 2000; Morrison and Williams 1968; Reber 2011; Snodgrass 2000; Schweitzer 1971; Zafeiropoulou 1983; 2001; and 2003; Zafeiropoulou and Agelarakis 2005).

Hence, data that may offer reflections on features and nuances of the circumstances and living conditions of populations which were active during this important temporal juncture are essential in providing comprehensive understandings of the time period dynamics; particularly when it may be possible to retrieve, study, and evaluate life aspects of the individual members[1] of those populations. Such an approach based on archaeological anthropology offers valuable research applications providing, in addition to bioarchaeological data, aspects on the subtleties of individual members' life hues and conditions, components of the communal dynamics and actions which facilitated transformations that in effect created the foundation pillars, the visions, and legacies of the Geometric period, thus also providing launching platforms for the modes of the subsequent Archaic period in Greek antiquity.

This report aims to offer glimpses of the human condition on Naxos island focusing on the archaeo-anthropologic study of the human skeletal remains along with associated contexts of faunal materials recovered from the Geometric (900 -700 BC) component of the burial ground site of *Plithos* in *Chora* at Naxos island. The record of skeletal remains was recovered mainly during the late 1970s with some additional materials unearthed in 2002 (Reber and Zapheiropoulou 2012; Zafeiropoulou 1988; and 2007). As provided by assessments of the anthropological laboratory study, carried out at the Naxos Archaeological Museum in 2005, the human skeletal population sample was identified to comprise 60 individuals[2], along with an associated assembly of faunal remains; see **Table 1** for a concise report. The human skeletal record had been recovered as primary and secondary burials, in inhumed or in cremated form, representing 48 burial contexts that involved either individual or multiple interments. Of the 60 human individuals identified during the laboratory analysis, four were atypically featured by few fragmented small infracranial bone fragments, or by a single *ex situ* tooth in dry form, while one in cremated form was represented by a flaked off bone fragment weighing 1.0gr[3]. While the recorded fragments representing these 5 individuals could be considered as of intrusive nature into the specific burial contexts from which they were recovered, juxtaposed to population approach assessments of the skeletal collection recovered, and based on their extremely limited condition of preservation as well as lack of further diagnostic anatomic criteria were not involved in subsequent inspectional and mensurational bioarchaeological analyses, or in palaeopathological assessments. Hence, the data of the skeletal record were retrieved from the remaining fifty-five individuals, while the unit of analysis in this project was based on the skeletal individual.

---

[1] In the case of this study from data permanently recorded on the human skeletal record of the ancients, and information gathered through the traces of their "fossilized" ideational world and behavioral conduct, imprinted and relatively safely preserved in the complex strata of their burial grounds.
[2] The analysis of the anthropological remains was carried out at a provisional laboratory space adjoining the museum's repository area. The author was assisted by a team of four students, namely: Angela Hernandez, Jessie Blackwood, Anna Sardis, and Sevasti M. Agelarakis.
[3] Of the five cases, those that were represented by axial or appendicular skeletal fragments, their maximum diameters ranged from 28.7mm to 43.76mm.

Analyses of the human skeletal record were carried out through the interdisciplinary methodological processes of BioArchaeology and Physical/Forensic Anthropology, following a protocol guided by the requirements of an Archaeological Anthropology laboratory substrate, in working with the unique, non-renewable, remains of the site's human skeletal record (Agelarakis 1996; Angel 1981; Aufderheide, Rodriguez-Martin, and Langsjoen 1998; Bass 2005; Brothwell 1981; Buikstra and Beck 2006; Hillson 2002; Iscan and Kennedy 1989; Komar and Buikstra 2008; Krogman, and Iscan 1986; Larsen 1997; Ortner 2003; Ortner and Putschard 1981; Shipman, Walker, and Bichell 1985; Steele and Bramblett 1988; Ubelaker 1982, and 1999; Wells 1960; White and Folkens 1991). Henceforth, primary focus was placed in the domain of skeletal biology through the arc trajectory of growth and development to degenerative and aging processes, the manifestations of anatomic morphology and epigenetic/non-metric variability, the nature of demographic composition dynamics, the composite of the palaeopathological profile, along with the tangible traces unveiled through the osteological study reflective of burial customs and practices; constituent elements as these may be in a reassembling of ingredients of life-milieus and of concepts on the passing to afterlife during the Geometric period at Naxos.

Geometric Component Burial Contexts and Anthropological Remains

Archaeological excavations at the Geometric component of the burial ground documented 48 burial contexts. The laboratory study of the anthropological record determined that 43 out of the 48 burial contexts that yielded human burials had involved single interments while 5 had contained multiple interments (**Graph 1**). These comprised an assemblage of 55 human individuals given that in addition to the 43 single individuals, 12 individuals were identified from the 5 burial contexts which involved multiple interments (**Graph 2**). One of those 5 burial contexts included 4 interments; the remaining 4 burial contexts involved 2 interments respectively. The latter appeared during the early stages of laboratory analysis to reveal a rather non-random condition, possibly featuring aspects of burial practice patterns. It was therefore rendered prudent to conceivably establish through the results of the anthropologic analysis the presence or absence of nuances of distinction or variability between the individuals that had been interred as single versus those of multiple interments; it was hypothesized that a set of data could have been yielded, conceivably instrumental in helping illuminate additional facets of the archaeo-anthropological study.

The skeletal population sample of 55 human individuals (*homini*) contained anthropological remains in both dry and cremated form. The 43 individuals yielded from burial contexts that involved single interments revealed a nearly isometric distribution ratio of 22:21 (51.16% : 48.84%) between dry and cremated anthropological remains while of the 12 interments retrieved from burial contexts that yielded multiple interments, 7 (58.33%) were in dry and 5 (41.67%) in cremated form. Hence, the skeletal collection of 55 individuals involved 29 (52.73%) dry, and 26 (47.27%) cremated individuals (**Graph 3**). The distribution of the 29 individuals interred in dry form, recovered from both burial contexts of single and multiple interments, comprised 9 infants and individuals of incomplete skeletal biological-development and maturation at the incidence of death which were designated as of "Indeterminate" biological sex, along with all 14 individuals within the cluster[4] of Females, and 6 individuals within the cluster of Males. Regarding the distribution of the 26 *homini* interred in cremated form, it clearly appears that the burial practice involved individuals which were assessed within the cluster of the male biological sex [25 (96.15%) out of 26 cases] with the exception of a case (3.85%) of an adult individual, of "Indeterminate" biological sex due to the very poor condition of skeletal preservation (**Table 2**).

---

[4] A biological sex assessment "cluster" may indicate the level of certainty of the assessment, for this particular project mainly based on the level of preservation of diagnostic anatomic morphologic criteria and/or availability of metric indicia documentation. Hence, similarly to a "male cluster", the "female cluster" includes for this project assessment rubrics such as "Females", "Probable Females", and "Possible Females". Where based on young age (as in Infancy), immature skeletal development, and/or poorly preserved skeletal remains hindering the retrieval of morphometric diagnostic data the biological sex assessment rubric designated was "Indeterminate".

Anatomic Distribution of Preserved Skeletal Remains

A variety of 9 prescribed subcategories were designated to characterize the nature of skeletal anatomic composition of the collection, annotating a site specific variability on the condition of preservation of the anthropological remains, reflective as it may be of burial customs and practices, as well as of diachronic processes and circumstances including bioturbation which had afforded physical and chemical changes on skeletal anatomic associations, and on individual dental, as well as on bone components within the taphonomic environment of the burial ground.

In addressing skeletal and anatomic representation among the 43 individuals (in both dry and cremated form) retrieved from burial contexts that yielded single interments, 15 (34.88%) individuals comprised both cranial, dental, post cranial axial, and post cranial appendicular remains, thus presenting the highest score among the ten prescribed subcategories on the curve of skeletal anatomic preservation, followed by the next subcategory comprising 7 (16.27%) individuals preserving postcranial appendicular remains. These were trailed by 8 successive subcategories tapering off at the prevalence score of 2.32% on skeleton-anatomic preservation, representing a single individual that had preserved post cranial axial and appendicular remains (**Graph 4**).

Regarding the skeletal preservation among the 12 individuals (of both dry and cremated form) retrieved from burial contexts that yielded multiple interments, 6 (50.00%) individuals comprising of cranial, post cranial axial and postcranial appendicular remains presented the apex on the curve, followed by 2 individuals (16.67%) preserving postcranial axial and appendicular remains, subsequently tapering off through four contiguous in prevalence subcategories involving 1 (8.33%) individual respectively (**Graph 5**).

In juxtaposing the measures of skeletal preservation and degree of anatomic representation of dental and skeletal surfaces between burial contexts which yielded single versus multiple interments, it clearly appears that the former fared better in this regard. Considering that there had not been any particular spatial distribution within the burial ground of graves holding single versus multiple interments, so as to suggest selective pressures of taphonomic impacts, yet without barring the effects of additional post-interment parameters of the natural environment (such as seasonal abiotic conditions of humidity, water level changes, and/or inundation), it is suggested that the reopening and reuse of those graves that received a second interment (with the exception of an unknown case(s) where the burial of multiple individuals took place at conterminous junctures) impacted the skeletal preservation of the earlier interment by altering, at a minimum, the geodynamic conditions *ante* in relation to the anthropological remains. Such changes alone could have afforded considerable deterioration to human remains, under any phase toward a state of stabilizing equilibrium the anthropological remains may have attained with the surrounding sediments and overall burial environment (Agelarakis 2014; Devlin and Herrmann 2015; Haglund and Sorg 1997). Emphasis to the latter provided the results of sediment acerbity in the burial ground, based on a selective sampling process of burial deposit analyses carried out by the anthropology team; these had revealed a chemical environment of relative acidity. This was an overall unfavorable attribute of the burial environment in the mode of preservation of human skeletal remains in either dry or cremated form. In fact it was reflective of the rather poor condition of preservation of all dental and bone surfaces recovered, indiscriminately between burial contexts of single versus multiple interments, particularly of the dry remains, given that considerable physical and chemical modifications are afforded on cremated dental and bone components prior to interment, initiating during pyre exposure (Bohnert, Rost and Pollak 1998; Buikstra and Swegle 1989; Gejvall 1969; Muller et al., 1998; Myers, Williams and Hodges 1999; Shipman, Foster and Schoeninger 1984; Thompson 2004; and 2005). The human cremated remains showed a mean value on the degree of thermal alteration sustained at a range between the "subcalcined",[5]

---

[5] Hue and chroma variables of Munsell readings of cremated bone surfaces, at the "subcalcined" level ranged between N 6.5/, 5Y 7.5/1, 2.5Y 7.5/0, 10YR 7.5/1.5, 7.5YR 7.5/0, and 5YR 7.5/1 (Munsell Color Company, 2000).

and more rarely at the "calcined"[6] level (Chochol 1961; Malinowski and Porawski 1969; Wahl 1983). The so called calcined degree of thermal alteration may represent the highest degree of funerary cremation changes on human bones in antiquity, reaching temperatures between >800° to ca. 1000°C whereby the organic-collagenous/protein components of bones would have been thermally obliterated (Push et al., 2000).

In considering, however, the configuration of skeletal preservation and anatomic representation of the collection at large, comprised of 55 *homini*, the highest cluster was scored by 16 (29.09%) interments which retained cranial, dental, post cranial axial, and post cranial appendicular remains, followed by 12 (21.815%) individuals with cranial, post cranial axial and post cranial appendicular remains, subsequently by 8 (14.54%) individuals with just postcranial appendicular remains, 6 (10.90%) individuals with only cranial remains, and successively tapering off toward the lowest prevalence score shared by three subcategories, each representing 2 (3.63%) individuals (**Graph 6**).

Aspects of Population Sample Demographic Profile

Evaluations of anatomic morphology and mensurational analyses of the skeletal individuals comprising the population sample were conducted through the scope of Physical/Forensic Anthropology methods and protocols, regarding the retrieval of data on the range of biological growth and maturation processes, reflections of biocultural adaptations permanently recorded on dental and bone surfaces, of acquired, degenerative, and aging changes in order to assess aspects of demographic composition dynamics on biological sex and age subgroups (Gejvall 1963; Graw, Wahl, and Ahlbrecht 2005; Jankauskas, Barakauskas and Bojarun 2001; Norèn et al., 2005; van Vark 1974; and 1975).

Biological Sex Assessments

Based on the level of assessment certainty[7], considering among other limiting parameters the state of dental and bone preservation per skeletal individual, seven subcategories have been designated to categorize biological sex determinations (**Table 2**), among the 55 individuals comprising the collection[8].

In cases where biological sex could be determined, it was documented that the majority of "Males" were identified as having been interred in cremated form, whereas "Females", and individuals designated within the "Indeterminate" biological sex subcategory[9] were retrieved in dry form. Addressing the composition of biological sex among the group of 43 individuals, retrieved from burial contexts which yielded single interments, Males comprised 46.51%, Females 23.25%, the "Indeterminate" subcategory 16.28%, followed at an isometric 4.65% between "Probable Females" and "Probable Males", and tapering off at 2.32% among the "Possible Females" and "Possible Males" respectively (**Graph 7**).

Regarding the 12 individuals retrieved from burial contexts which yielded multiple interments, the majority were Males (50.0%), followed by the "Indeterminate" subcategory (25.0%), and successively culminating with Females, Probable Males and Possible Males at 8.33% respectively (**Graph 8**). Hence, it appeared that Males dominated the synthesis of individuals interred in burial contexts which yielded single interments, followed by Females and chiefly tapering off with the "Indeterminate" subcategory. Among the burial contexts which yielded multiple interments Males were more prevalent, followed by the "Indeterminate" subgroup and tapering off with Females; hence Males showed in both cases the greatest

---

[6] Hue and chroma variables of Munsell readings of cremated bone surfaces at the "calcined" level ranged between 5Y 8/1, 10YR 8/1.5, and 5YR 8/1.
[7] Centered in the study of morphologic anatomy and mensurational analyses.
[8] The core sample of the collection excluded the five cases as described in footnote 3, *supra*.
[9] As explained above, this subcategory was designated to include either young in age individuals with immaturely developed skeletal bodies, and/or individuals that showed poorly preserved bone surfaces and structures whereby morpho-anatomic and mensurational evaluations could not substantiate a relative forensic assessment.

prevalence while Females and "Indeterminate" reversed positions between the two groups of single versus multiple interments (**Graph 9**). In fact, the ensemble of the 55 individuals comprising this population sample, lumped in correlating aggregates on the male, and female biological sex assessment accounted for an 56.36% proportionality for the Males and 25.45% for Females; therefore, Females were only represented at the 45.16th percentile of the Male prevalence. The "Indeterminate" subcategory equated to 18.18% of the population sample (**Graph 10**).

Age Assessments

Similarly to the methodological processes implemented for the biological sex assessments, considering the level of assessment certainty, twelve subcategories (**Table 3**) were designated, interweaving where appropriate between the boundaries of eight basic age categories (**Table 4**), for establishing age determinations among the 55 individuals of the collection.

The better state of skeletal preservation among individuals recovered from burial contexts which yielded single interments presented fewer limiting parameters in age assessment processes compared to the group of the burial contexts which yielded multiple interments. Regarding the latter, it should be of interest to note that the composition of interments in each of those 5 burial contexts consisted in 3 out of the 5 cases by a skeletally mature Male individual paired with an infant, in the fourth case by three skeletally mature Male individuals and an infant, while the fifth case included a mature Male and a Female individual. Hence, in sequence of interment biological sex and age prevalence herein, there were 7 Males, 4 infants, and 1 Female.

Referring to the age at death variability documented among the 43 individuals retrieved from burial contexts which yielded single interments, all twelve age subcategories[10] were designated depicting a mortality curve initiating at early post natal years, within "Infancy I", through to old age, within the "Older or *Senilis*"(**Graph 11**). An integration of the twelve age at death subcategories, as illustrated in an abridged version of the eight basic age subgroups, clearly reveals a greater mortality prevalence clustering among three sequential age subcategories of Adulthood[11], cresting within Middle Adulthood[12] (**Graph 12**). In further evaluating the intra-age at death dynamics of this group of single interments, the isomerous values documented within "Infancy I" and "Infancy II", initiate an ascending course on a curve depicting an increase of loss of life, by a 25% proportionality, during the next age subgroup of "Subadulthood", reflective of aspects of demographic attrition during the adolescent years of life, while the range of subsequent years, within "Young Adulthood", show the greatest sequential increase of mortality prevalence between age subcategories, by a nearly two and a half times increase[13], then further ascending to the apex scored during "Middle Adulthood", subsequently diminishing during "Late Adulthood", at a relevant measure to "Young Adulthood", and thereafter most drastically tapering off, by more than eighteen times toward the "*Maturus*", and the "Older" age subgroup years (**Graph 13**).

In regards to the age at death variability documented among the 12 individuals retrieved from burial contexts which yielded multiple interments, six of the twelve age subcategorizations[14] were designated depicting a mortality curve initiating at early post natal years through to "Late Adulthood", presenting a number of variabilities to what was documented among the individuals recovered from burial contexts

---

[10] See table of Graph 11.
[11] Young Adulthood, Middle Adulthood, and Late Adulthood.
[12] In the lumped version of the eight basic age categories a proportional distribution to the three Adulthood age subcategories was implemented from the initial, detailed, age subcategories such as those of the "SubAdults-Young Adults" (abbreviated in Graph 11 as SAYA), the "Young-Middle Adulthood" (YAMA), the "Middle-Late Adulthood" (MALA), the "General Adulthood" (GA), and the "Late Adulthood-*Maturus*" (LAM).
[13] The "SubAdult" score reached only to the level of 40.7% of the "Young Adult" mortality prevalence.
[14] These comprised six of the twelve subcategorizations which were used to designate detailed age at death assessments among the individuals retrieved from burial contexts with single interments; see Footnote 10, *supra*.

with single interments (**Graph 14**). A review of the six age at death subcategorizations compiled in an abridged form involved only five of the eight basic age subgroups (**Table 4**) revealing the traces nevertheless of an non-continuous sigmoidal curve (**Graph 15**). In this particular group of the multiple interments the template of mortality curve, even if though when evaluated for a qualitative review, was rather initiated within "Infancy I", indicative of population attrition in the early years of life, subsequently sharply diminishing, by a threefold, during the "Infancy II", and absolving during "Subadulthood"; showing herein an improved survivorship during those two later age subcategories compared to the single interments' group. Subsequently, mortality prevalence ascended within the "Young Adulthood" years, at a predominance that simulated the proportionality documented among the group of the single interments, cresting during the "Middle Adulthood" years, and subsequently decreasing during "Late Adulthood", thus simulating in these loci the curve of the single interments' group; however differing from it by lacking any representation in the cohorts of the "Maturus" and "Older" age subgroups (**Graph 16**).

A rather detailed age at death distribution among the entire sample of 55 individuals, combining both groups of single and multiple interments are shown in **Graph 17**, appropriately providing the dynamics of numeric prevalence and percentage values per subcategory. An abridged version of the previous, depicting the score values analogous to eight basic age subgroups (**Graph 18**) reflects on a sigmoid-shaped curve whereby the earliest juncture of population attrition initiates in moderate ways within "Infancy I", abating during "Infancy II" and "SubAdulthood", subsequently increasing within "Young Adulthood", to crest in "Middle Adulthood", and then to sharply taper off at the "Maturus"/"Older" cohorts.

Surpassing the more dangerous early years of life during "Infancy I", often characterized by the potential of increased morbidity and mortality (from a range of conditions imposed i.e. from weanling diarrhea to communicable/infectious childhood diseases), the "Infancy II" and "SubAdult" age subgroups seem to have fared better in survivorship ability. This is suggested to have been based among other parameters on matters of available cultural buffer mechanisms to alleviate physiological and pathological stress during those critical years of biological growth and development. Thus, the sharply ascending mortality prevalence sustained past "Subadulthood", namely within "Young Adulthood", the successive cresting during "Middle Adulthood", and it's still considerable although somewhat abating prevalence within "Late Adulthood" (with the exception of a case(s) of epidemic) could be revealing of the highly demanding and taxing responsibilities and on the anatomic and physiological burden placed on those age subgroups on matters of obligations and dependability of both private matters and interests, and of communal mandates required or exacted on the membership of the cohorts involved. In reference to the drastically diminishing prevalence of morbidity by nearly an eight- fold, among the "*Maturus*" and "Older" cohorts combined, it is assessed it may rather be characteristic of the diminished, if not improbable, potential for the majority of the population membership to extended longevity and survivorship to old age (**Graph 19**). Apropos, in a synthesis that were to further abridge the population membership of the two Infancy and SubAdult age cohorts, representative of the precarious years (from birth to <18 years) during active biological growth and developmental processes, critical for population growth dynamics, sustainability, and strength in genealogical succession, the mortality prevalence scored a formidable range of 25%, whereas population attrition reached the daunting range of a 78% prevalence during the combined "Adulthood" age cohorts (within a range of 27 years, that is from 18 to 45 years); hence leaving only a feeble less than 3% of the combined survivorship scores to the "*Maturus*" and "Older" age cohorts (a chronological range from 45+ to 65+ years).

The mortality prevalence by age subgroup of the Naxian population sample, reflective as it may be of a random subset of their demographic dynamic, directs one to cogitate on the complex ensemble of site specific conditions and parameters coeval to the time period that could and would have pertained to it. Such conditions reflective of their realm of life, it is suggested, would involve a multitude of aspects ranging from the sphere of the population's gene pool attributes to the macro-horizon of conditions relative to the dimensions of their physical environment and territorial expanse, the domain of their socio-cultural and political organizational abilities and mandates, as well as of their techno-economical capacities implemented, to mention a few.

On Skeletal Morphology

Seeking to better decipher aspects of life conditions permanently recorded on the skeletal record of the population sample, despite the limiting parameters imposed by preservation issues, emphasis was placed on inspectional evaluations indicative of *ante mortem* biological growth, development, and maturation, as well as of degenerative processes due to aging and pathogenesis. Emphasis was placed in the identification of non-metric and mensurational features of skeletal changes reflective of population specific acclimatizations, adaptability issues, and intra-population variability on matters of skeletomuscular build and robustness, labor diversity issues by age or biological age subgroup, and of the realm of traceable kinetics in physical activities showing skeletomuscular changes as markers of habitual and/or occupational stress (Agelarakis 1996a). The latter mainly represented cranio-infracranial skeleto-anatomic loci where ligamento-muscular attachments of origin and insertion, of muscles that functioned in synergistic and/or antagonistic ways, had left emphasized skeletal imprints. These bone marks are a consequence of *ante mortem* skeleto-muscular actions which had caused modifications and enhancement of the bone substrate through plasticity changes as had been required by the particulars of life modes[15]; although more rarely it may be possible to palaeopathologically document cases of musculo-skeletal trauma in a variety of phases during the healing process.

During this multifaceted stage of analysis, as with the age and biological sex assessments, the group of individuals recovered as single interments was initially examined as a population subgroup to be compared with data yielded from the subgroup of individuals recovered as multiple interments. This was carried out as a precaution against any presumptions, considering that the observed variability in the particulars of the burial praxis and customs could yield (or even not yield), through forensic anthropologic analysis, additional data in favor of the archaeo-anthropologic investigation.

Out of the group of single interments comprising 43 *homini*, 17 (39.33%) individuals were either not adequately preserved or were representing, due to young age, immaturely developed skeletal bodies for such a study. The remaining 26 (60.47%) individuals showed adequately preserved skeletal surfaces pertinent for studies in morphologic anatomy. Of those, 18 individuals showed manifestations of skeletal robustness and/or particular features of emphasized skeletomuscular changes, whereas the remaining 8 individuals lacked an emphasis in such skeletal features; the latter were assessed as of a gracile skeletomuscular build (**Graph 20**). The specific composition of these three morphologic anatomy subgroups, regarding the mode of their interment between inhumation and cremation, of the biological sex and age subgroup distribution appears as follows. The non-adequately preserved, for said analysis, subgroup of 17 individuals comprised 8 cremations and 2 inhumations of adults, and 7 inhumations of skeletally immature as well as poorly preserved *homini*. The subgroup of the 8 individuals assessed as of a gracile skeletal build comprised 4 cremated adult males and 4 inhumed adult females. Finally the subgroup of 18 individuals that showed emphasized skeleto-muscular manifestations consisted of 9 cremated adult males and 9 inhumed adult females (**Graph 20a**).

Henceforth, of the subgroup of 18 individuals, all 18 showed some form of skeletomuscular robustness, 17 of which revealed traces of tangible bone plasticity changes in loci of muscular origin and insertions, particularly on the appendicular skeletal structures relevant to a prevalent specificity of kinetic *in vivo*

---

[15] Such bone changes may be caused by passive or specific, even idiosyncratic in nature, long term, repeated actions, affording conditions of trajectory stress by *ante mortem* kinetics in activities which had been either habitual or required of the individual(s) involved.

actions, designated as markers of habitual and/or occupational stress (MHOS); yet 5 of those individuals revealed a combination of considerable manifestations of overall robustness in skeletal build in addition to significantly enhanced loci of muscular origin and insertions in structures of the appendicular skeleton (**Graph 21**). Further, regarding the documented prevalence of some form of skeletomuscular robustness within this subgroup, a 100% observation ratio was discerned, involving all 18 adult individuals (of both female and male biological sex). Of the 17 of them that showed skeletomuscular markers characterized as MHOS, 8 were cremated males and 9 were inhumed females; the 5 individuals which combined skeletomuscular markers of MHOS along with overall skeletal robustness comprised 4 cremated males and one inhumed female (**Graph 21a**).

Of the group of 12 homini representing the multiple interments, 2 adult individuals (16.67%) were preserved in an inadequate state of preservation, whereas the remaining 10 (83.33%) showed adequate skeletal surfaces for evaluations of morphologic anatomy. Of the latter, 6 individuals showed manifestations of skeletal robustness and/or particular features of emphasized skeletomuscular changes whereas 4 individuals lacked an emphasis in such skeletal features due to their very young age and hence of immature skeletal development (**Graph 22**). The composition of the three morphologic anatomy subgroups described above, regarding the mode of their interment between inhumation and cremation, and of their biological sex and age subgroup distribution appears as follows. The non-adequately preserved subgroup comprised 2 inhumations of an adult male and female individual in a very poor state of preservation. Of the subgroup of the 4 individuals of immature skeletal development, interred in dry form, 3 were of the "Infancy I", and 1 of the "Infancy II" age cohorts. Finally the subgroup of 6 individuals that showed emphasized skeletomuscular manifestations consisted of male individuals, 5 in cremated and 1 in dry form (**Graph 22a**).

Regarding the subgroup of 6 male individuals, all showed some form of skeletomuscular robustness in body build. With the exception of one of those individuals, whereby the appendicular skeletal surfaces were not well preserved for further analyses, the remaining 5 males showed a combination of considerable manifestations of robustness in skeletal build and significantly enhanced loci of muscular origin and insertions, MHOS, in structures of the appendicular skeleton, relevant to prevalent kinetic actions carried out *ante mortem* (**Graph 23**). While features of some form of skeletomuscular robustness within this subgroup of male individuals showed a 100% observation ratio, their age subgroup distribution ranged from "Young Adulthood" to "Late Adulthood", and of the 5 of them that showed MHOS changes, having retained appendicular surfaces, the Late Adult had been inhumed while the rest had been cremated (**Graph 23a**).

Henceforward, in considering features of morphologic anatomy with a focus on robustness of skeletal build along with skeletomuscular markers among both groups of the individuals representing the single versus those of the multiple interments, 24 individuals were documented to reveal such manifestations, whereas 12 individuals lacked them[16]; the remaining 19 individuals had shown inadequate skeletal preservation (**Graph 24**). Further, it clearly appeared in comparing the 36 individuals of the two groups[17], those of the multiple interments comprised a proportionally greater number of individuals which showed adequately preserved skeletal surfaces for studies in morphologic anatomy at a rate of 83.33% compared to 60.47% of the individuals of single interments.

Although regarding the overall representation of dental and skeletal remains (on matters of general preservation of the anthropological remains) the individuals from the group of single interments fared better compared to the group of multiple interments, as explained above, the study and evaluations of

---

[16] This subgroup comprised 8 individuals of the single interments (4 cremated males consisting of 1 "SubAdult", 2 "Middle Adults", and 1 "Late Adult"; 1 inhumed "Late Adult/Maturus" male; and 3 inhumed females consisting of 1 "SubAdult", 1 "Young Adult/Middle Adult", and 1 "General Adult"), and 4 individuals of the multiple interments (3 in "Infancy I", and 1 in "Infancy II").

[17] The combined subsets of : a) 24 individuals documented to reveal skeleton-anatomic manifestations of robustness and MHOS changes, along with b) the 12 individuals that lacked them.

skeletal anatomic morphology (also a matter subject to the realm of preservation of anthropological remains) depended on discrete preservation parameters. It was not merely the quantitative completeness of the skeletal representation of each individual unearthed that critically contributed to the subject matter at hand. Equally important for the study of morphologic anatomy was the quality of preservation of clinical and anatomic dental surfaces, and of the skeletal components their ectosteal surfaces preserving and clearly revealing diagnostic loci, features, and manifestations pertinent to the study of anatomic morphology.

In continuing with the intra-site evaluation of morphologic anatomy features juxtaposed between the groups of single versus multiple interments[18] (**Graph 24**), the subset of 6 individuals of the group of multiple interments superseded by a 1.19 ratio (50% : 41.86%) the prevalence in adequate skeletal preservation with observed manifestations of robustness and MHOS the subset of 18 individuals of the group of single interments[19]. Yet, the latter subset revealed among its constituent members an overwhelming (94.44%) prevalence of MHOS changes while they were lacking an overall robust skeletal build; in relation to 27.8% which showed robust skeletal build along with MHOS markers. This was ostensibly variable to the subset of the multiple interments which showed an 100% prevalence in overall robustness in skeletal build, in relation to 83.33% that showed prevalence of combined MHOS markers along with overall robustness in skeletal build (**Graph 25**). It should be of interest to note that among both groups, of single versus multiple interments, a respective subgroup of 5 male individuals, that in both cases had been interred in cremated form, were observed to have presented the most robust skeletal build and emphasized skeleto-muscular markers compared to the rest of the adult individuals of the entire skeletal collection.

With regards to the population sample morphologic anatomy features, it was apparent that males from both groups of the single and the multiple interments revealed a more robust skeletal body build than females in reference to their infracranial axial and appendicular skeletal structures and with emphasis on skeletomuscular changes. Yet it clearly appears that while females may have been buffered from required exposure to excessively demanding physical activities, particularly as it may have concerned trajectory forces of stress during load bearing activities, they were not in fact lacking in skeletomuscular changes on the lower extremities which were indicative of most frequent *ante mortem* involvement in extensive locomotory behavior in nearly precipitous substrates; while in matters of a particular body posture, the squatting position was documented to predominate with knee joint hyperflexion along with hyperextension of the hip joints.

Apropos, regarding a manifestation exclusively observed among several female individuals (and of at least one suspected female individual within the Infancy II age subcategory), members of the single interment group, ranging in age cohorts at the occurrence of death from "SubAdulthood" to "Middle Adulthood", showed at their cranial vault bones a continuously smooth yet discernibly well-defined form of post-coronal depression, running from the vertex bilaterally along the lateral walls of the parietals and fading bilaterally at the approximate region of the inferior temporal line of M. *temporalis*. The manifestation, it is suggested, could be explained along the lines of gender based variability, as the consequence of a band of webbing worn since infantile years, synchronous with the developmental formation of the *calvaria* and neurocranium; it would have strapped over the particular domain of the head affording benign compression effects between the juncture of the coronoid suture to the anterior parietal eminences. Hence, it is assessed that the post-coronal depression was the result of a head-attire worn for both functional-utilitarian purposes and/or for aesthetic reasons rather than for an intentional artificial deformation of the head, given the inconspicuous morphological changes that would have been afforded *in vivo*.

Further on female prevalence of skeletomuscular changes at loci of muscular origin and insertion, their upper extremities indicated long term, copious skeletomuscular systems' actions which had involved

---

[18] Even if for qualitative purposes.
[19] Values calculated after making the relative fractions proportional among the respective groups.

scapulo-humero-clavicular, synergetic in nature kinetics in extension/flexion and abduction/adduction movements of the upper arms with elbows in flexion-extension modes along with wrist rotatory actions, and with significant strength in the flexion ability of hand phalanges. Incidentally, males also revealed similar upper extremity skeletomuscular changes, however with greater prominence, particularly at the muscular attachments of the Ms. *deltoideus* and *trapezius*. These, as an allotted portion of their respective function, strengthen and secure the humero-scapular joint during substantial load-bearing actions and particularly while the encumbrance of the burden is amplified by the upper arms held in transverse extension, positioned forwardly and laterally from the body's axial center of gravity[20]. Consistent to the latter, among males, were their strongly emphasized muscular attachments at the M. *supraspinatus* that offers antigravity stamina in the abduction and rotation of the arm, stabilizing the shoulder joint, before the engagement of M. *deltoideus* in contributing synergistically further strength and stamina to the ongoing kinetic action. Further, unlike females, males indicated a robust emphasis on the combination of skeletomuscular changes at the occipito-nuchal and infra-nuchal regions indicative of strength in head and neck ipsilateral and contralateral as well as forward movements in combination with the sterno-clavicular areas, the spine (with emphasis at the cervical domain), as well as the shoulder blades. Particularly in the shoulder blades there were emphasized imprints observed at the loci of attachment of M. *triceps brachii*. The latter, while adducting the shoulder extends the elbow joint, which combined with traces of robust imprint changes documented at the *M. brachialis* would have powerfully aided in the flexion of the elbow joints. Additionally, on the scapular splanchnic surface, robust imprints of M. *subscapularis* indicated supplementary support to arm kinetic functions in mesio-rotatory actions of the humerus in extension, and in forward as well as supero-inferior movements while also securing the stability (against dislocation) of the shoulder joint.

Females in addition to their moderately emphasized skeleto-muscular imprints of the upper arm bones, conditions which simulated male imprints, showed a particular predilection in the humeral domains of attachment of Ms. *latissimus dorsi* that extends, adducts, and internally rotates the upper arm, the medial head of M. *triceps brachii* that extends the forearm at the elbow joint, M. *pronator teres* that abducts and flexes the wrist, Ms. *flexor carpi radialis* and *ulnaris*, which abduct, adduct, and flex the wrist, M. *flexor digitorum superficialis* that flexes the fingers, as also attested by the radial diaphyseal imprints of the later, and further substantiated by the ulnar imprints of M. *flexor digitorum profundus* that flexes the interphalangeal joints of the hand.

Whereas a considerable number of physical activities may implicate the kinetic actions of the upper extremities as documented among females, it is suggested that we may be witnessing traces of long term labor intensive aspects, revealing of a thorough participation in economic output process, possibly in activities required in agriculture, in the processes that simulate the milking of domesticates, yet particularly in the spinning and making of thread and of the weaving process in the vertical and/or horizontal loom, to mention a few. On the other hand, traces of male activities may be reconstructed, which among a plethora of heavier load impact tasks required could include, it is suggested, intensive work in agricultural activities, and particularly in seafaring with emphasis in the stamina and dexterity required in power-rowing.

Lending support to the latter on the demanding physical activities and tasks required by the male individuals were lower extremity manifestations showing imprint traces from the iliac crests of the innominate bones with emphasis on the M. *obliquus externus abdominis* that compresses the chest area and slightly rotates the torso contralaterally, M. *transversus abdominis* that both compresses the abdomen and aids in lifting the body assuming the action to buffer vertebral column vertical pressure, as in cases of heavy load-bearing, while M. *obliquus internus abdominis* compresses the abdomen and aids in the

---

[20] Also attested by emphasis on M. *infraspinatus* attachments.

ipsilateral rotation of the spine. Similarly, the ensemble of femoral muscle attachments that extended and both rotated as well as adducted the hip joint, in standing, walking and running acts, the involvement of the abduction, flexion, extension and slight rotation of the legs, the stability and flexion of knee joints, were most emphasized. Tibio-fibular muscular imprints further substantiated robustly featured muscular imprints for the hip flexion, knee extension and stabilization, plantar-, and dorsi-flexion of the feet in both inversion and eversion, all indicative of extensive *ante mortem* courses of bipedal locomotory behavior.

Additional lines of evidence in support of the inspectional morpho-anatomic evaluations which revealed that male individuals had developed and retrained robust body frames were mensurational data retrieved from the cremated remains (cremains), given that the majority of the male individuals had been cremated. These, representing 27 male individuals, comprised metric indicia of a select number of 313 well preserved cremains from the cranial vault and appendicular-tubular bone fragments[21] yielding an abridged cranio-infracranial appendicular statistical bone thickness average of 5.571789 mm (**Graph 26**). The score of the average value offered evidentiary data corroborating the inspectional morpho-anatomic evaluations and further substantiating the assessment indicative of the well developed and robustly built skeletomuscular systems of the male individuals regarding their biological developmental growth processes[22]. Furthermore, in order to sustain and possibly even enhance the strong build of powerful body frames, multifactorial in nature, engaging, physically active life conditions indirectly refer to embracing of biological sex-specific cultural norms, responsibilities and directives, inclusive but not limited to aspects of gymnastics, military training and service, as well as of occupational requirements.

At an inter-site comparative context, the above mentioned bone metric average value supersedes relative average scores of the warrior aggregate interred in the Athenian Demosion Sema Polyandria (Agelarakis 2013), at 5.150643522mm[23], dating to the 5th c. BC, and of the Eleuthernian warriors from the Orthi Petra burial ground in Rethymnon, Crete, interred in the monumental tomb-*heroon* A1K1 (Agelarakis 2005), at 5.259928 mm [24], dating from approximately the end of the 9th to the very beginning of the 6th century BC, whereas it clusters below the lower proximity of the average scored by the warrior cremains of the Paros-Paroikia polyandria[25], dating from the lower third of the 8th to possibly the early years of the 7th century BC (Zafeiropoulou and Agelarakis 2005).

Palaeopathological Profile

Palaeopathologic Conditions

Further to *intra vitam* traces permanently recorded on the skeletal record, the palaeopathological profile of the population sample involved revealed aspects of the human condition, particularly on matters of acquired and degenerative disease, initially examined per group, namely of the individuals of single versus those of the multiple interments.

Based on the criteria of dental and skeletal surfaces' condition of preservation for conducting palaeopathological evaluations 14 (32.59%) of the 43 individuals of the single interments' group were excluded while 29 (67.44%) were selected for analysis. Twenty two of the latter were assessed to have been affected by disease discernible on the dental and skeletal surfaces, while the remaining 7 showed a

---

[21] These were selected based on their well-preserved ecto-endocranial, or ecto-endosteal long-bone components and surfaces.
[22] A domain inclusive of both genetic and congenital conditions, of developmental growth issues, as well as of physical and social environmental contexts and dynamics.
[23] Cf. Agelarakis, A., (2013). On the Anthropology Project of 35 Salaminos Street Site of Kerameikos, Athens: A Brief Account. Archaeologikés Symvolés, Volume B: Attika, A' and Γ' Prehistoric and Classical Antiquities Authorities, Museum of Cycladic Art, Athens, p: 380.
[24] Cf. Agelarakis, A., (2005). The Anthropology of Tomb A1K1 of Orthi Petra in Eleutherna: A Narrative of the Bones: Aspects of the Human Condition in Geometric-Archaic Eleutherna. University of Crete, Rethymnon, p: 45.
[25] Agelarakis, A., The Anthropology of the Paroikia Polyandreia of Paros Island. Manuscript in preparation.

lack of such pathological changes (**Graph 27**). Regarding the 12 individuals of the multiple interment group, 11 (91.67%) were selected for analysis of which 5 showed lack of disease manifestations on the dental and skeletal record (**Graph 28**). Comprising the sample membership in both groups were individuals of both biological sex subgroups at a range of age cohorts, as well as individuals that although had been assessed as "Indeterminate" for either age or sex subgroups determination, for lack of preserved diagnostic anatomic morphology, they nevertheless had preserved aspects of their dental and skeletal components sufficiently for retrieving evidence of palaeopathological changes.

Subsequently, the proportional relation between the individuals manifesting palaeopathologic changes among the single versus the multiple interment groups yielded a ratio of 51.16% versus 50.00% respectively[26]. Thus the proportional relation among the individuals that revealed palaeopathologic manifestations between the two groups seemed to lack prevalence variability, suggestive as it may be of a rather similar if not shared contextual environment for the possibilities of pathologic onset and/or of non-significant variability in the conditions that would engender the acquisition of infectious, traumatic, or degenerative in nature pathogenesis. The latter however could be skewed when considering that the proportional percentiles between the individuals not afflicted by disease, between the single versus the multiple interments groups, yielded a ratio of 16.28% versus 41.67%; seemingly indicating a 2.559 ratio in favor of the multiple interments' group to avoid disease manifestations such that would have been traceable on their dental and skeletal record. Providing a complicating parameter in the aim toward a better understanding of this intra-site investigation remained the disparity between the inadequately preserved skeletal individuals for palaeopathologic study of the single versus the multiple interment groups yielding a ratio of 32.59% to 8.33% respectively; the single interments' group exceeding by a 3.906 ratio their counterpart group, of individuals that remained excluded from palaeopathologic analysis[27]. Hence, it could be ostensibly stated that in reference to an observationally based correlation there was predominance in the overall prevalence of palaeopathological manifestations among the single compared to the multiple interments. In such cases where intra-site population subgroups' palaeopathologic evaluations are essential for retrieving additional forensic clues on the esoteric folds of their relational dynamics, emphasis may be placed in the particulars of the kind and type of causative agents of documented pathogenetic changes, and the nature of their distribution among the membership of said subgroups.

In **graphs 29 and 30**, a concise view may be presented of palaeopathological profile dynamics among the afflicted individuals of the two groups, with their respective distribution and prevalence per subcategory of pathological changes. In the proportional relations of the incidence of palaeopathologic manifestations among both groups ectocranial porosity clearly scores the greatest prevalence, sustained at 54.55% among the individuals of the single interment group, and at 100% among the individuals of the multiple interments group; the latter exceeding their counterpart group by a 1.833 ratio.

Regarding both groups, cranial palaeopathologic changes of ectocranial porosity manifestations, mostly of porotic and rarely of cribrotic sizes, chiefly affected the vault and lateral wall areas, and in fewer cases the intra-orbiral roof surfaces. These were mainly assessed as primary periosteal reactions, secondary responses to infectious (some of contagious nature) and inflammatory causative agents, as well as due to acquired complications[28] relative to anemias[29]. Porotic and in fewer cases hyperporotic changes had also affected, yet less frequently, endocranial surfaces; these manifestations were revealing of the morbidity potential of

---

[26] The relation of percentile values of observed palaeopathology manifestations among the single versus the multiple interment group revealed a ratio of 1.023, indicative of no significant statistical difference between them.
[27] And yet, counterpoints to the latter may be raised considering that four individuals of the multiple interment group would have had by the merit of their very young age a lack of degenerative in nature diseases.
[28] For example from metabolic imbalances, postpartum conditions for female individuals even if temporary but interrupted by the incidence of death, and even of alimentary tract parasitic infestation.
[29] Cases of pernicious, hereditary, anemias were rather not observed, taking in consideration the cranio-infracranial palaeopathologic changes observed, although in several of those cases evaluated among incompletely preserved skeletal individuals.

infectious/inflammatory conditions that had affected the meningeal domain. Diseases of jaws and teeth were documented in the form of periodontal disease diagnostically manifested with mild to rarely moderate supra-gingival calculus deposits, absorption of alveolar and interdental *septae* for the most part conducive to aging, alongside with continuous "eruption" of dental anatomical surfaces within the oral cavity. The greater prevalence of dental and periodontal disease manifestations diagnosed among the single interment group mainly relies in the domain of preservation given that in cases of cremation the dental arcades and the dental tissues[30] tend to succumb to the effects of thermal alteration during pyre exposure[31].

Traces of temporomandibular joint osteoarthitic changes documented exclusively among the aging were accompanied by discernible height reductions of the mandibular bodies, occasionally along with the flaring out of the mandibular angles (*gonion* loci) based on progressively modified, and intensified, demands on the muscles of mastication with emphasis at the attachments of Ms. masseters, but also of the mesial and lateral M. *pterygoidei*; particularly when posterior (buccal) teeth in the dental arcades had been lost long before the occurrence of death. Incidentally, whereas periapical abscesses were rare, a number of cariogenic lesions affecting interdental crown surfaces, had initiated their infectious lytic lesions at the cervical regions of the cemento-enamel junctions. Carious cavities were not widespread however on dental surfaces of the individuals involved, a good number of dental arches having not been affected at all. The low prevalence of cervical cariogenic lesions was indirectly revealing of a dietary intake partially based on agricultural products while indicating[32] a rather infrequent consumption of concentrated simple sugars derived as soluble carbohydrates (i.e. monosaccharides, glucose and fructose) from plants and/or honey, or (as galactose) from milk and relevant byproducts. Wear of dental incisal and occlusal surfaces revealed that the bulk of the foods consumed had been well prepared, whereas in several cases it was possible to document the preferable use of labial incisal surfaces in "third hand" functions, however without obliterating or severely modifying the proximal thirds of the dental clinical surfaces.

Apropos to *ante mortem* traces permanently imprinted on dental surfaces, enamel hypoplastic defects were documented in the form of sporadic pitting, and lines of arrested and improved growth. The study of the latter, coined as linear enamel hypoplasias (LEH), indicated conditions of early life systemic (corporeal) stress which temporarily arrested the growth of the sensitive enamel producing cells (enameloblasts) of the developing dental crowns; their function rebounded when the health of the individuals improved[33]. Hence, it was possible to record through mensurational LEH analyses that four temporal junctures within the range of "Infancy I" age subgroup would broadly represent biological age occasions of stress, affecting the membership of the population involved, namely at 2.5, 3.2, 4.2, and 5.0 years of age. The majority of individuals manifesting LEH were not affected during all biological age instances mentioned above, while the fact that all individuals affected by LEH survived the stress condition(s) reflects on a favorable survivorship trend; the latter mirrors on the ability of the socio-cultural system to have alleviated and buffered the occasions of both physiological-exterior, and pathologic stress when it affected a number of the very young of its membership. It should be noted, however that the near absence of dental pathologies (abbreviated as DP in **Graphs 29, and 30**) inclusive of cariogenic lesions and LEH among the group of multiple interments is chiefly based on the lack of adequate dental preservation and thus the inability for subsequent diagnostic assessments rather than that the said group was unaffected.

---

[30] Particularly the dental tissue of enamel along with at least the layer of mantle dentin which it superimposes, along with components of primary dentin which superimposes the pulp of cavity, further toward a cervical region involving the entire crown surface peripheral to the cemento-enamel junction.

[31] The effects are more drastic when higher temperatures are reached, identified when the skeletal record is affected to the levels of "subcalnined" and "calnined" degrees.

[32] Without excluding forms of dental hygiene/care by a number of the individuals involved.

[33] LEH causative agents affecting deciduous teeth may include prenatal conditions due to maternal health issues, and in postnatal circumstances, which also affected the permanent set of dentitions, physiological stress (i.e. environmental stressors causing seasonal under/malnutrition-starvation), cultural mandates (i.e. weanling diarrhea, and/or under nutrition/malnutrition) and/or pathological stress (i.e. trauma impact combined during recovery with inadequate dietary intake, fevers, infections-communicable diseases, etc.).

Post cranial palaeopathologic changes mainly involved periosteal changes of the appendicular structures and few cases of vertebral body height reduction due to aging processes. Post cranial pathologies appeared to have scored the second most prevalent conditions among both groups of single versus multiple interments (abbreviated as PCP in **Graphs 29, and 30**). Spondyloarthropathic changes (mainly degenerative, and in few cases secondary to compression trauma due of excessive loadbearing impact) reflected on infracranial axial skeletal manifestations[34], whereas osteoarthopathic changes, principally documented in the form of marginal lipping and relative articular surfaces' and facets' changes from porosity to post-osteoarthropathathic, sclerotic-necrotic (eburnated), conditions involved joints of the appendicular skeletal structures. Based on an observational correlation the group of single interments uniquely exceeded its counterpart group in the prevalence of spondyloarthropathies, and in osteoarthropathic changes by a ratio of 1.636 (**Graphs 29, and 30**). Further, conditions of appendicular articular surfaces' eburnation were exclusively observed among the group of single interments, indicative as it may be of long term most frequent use of those joints in specific actions required it is suggested by both cultural mandates and/or occupational parameters[35].

Evaluating the dynamics of the palaeopathological profile of both groups combined, 15 (27.27%) out of 55 individuals of the population sample could not be assessed due to preservation limitations, 12 (21.82%) individuals involved in the analysis showed no discernible dental or skeletal pathologic changes, while 28 (50.90%) had been affected revealing palaeopathologic manifestations (**Graph 31**). A considerable number of individuals from the latter subcategory typically showed more than one palaeopathologic manifestation on their dental and/or skeletal remains preserved; and rather of both associated and/or varied causative agents. As communicable disease is one of the major morbidity factors with the potential for mortality and thus population attrition, particularly among members of settled socio-cultural environmental contexts, the ostensibly high[36] incidence of 28 (50.90% prevalence) out of 55 individuals documented to have been affected by palaeopathological conditions may not be perceived, it is suggested, as an ominous characterization of the population's health status, or ability to buffer disease should one contemplate that a good number of the documented palaeopathologic manifestations had not been in themselves the cause of death nor had they been imminently life threatening to the individuals involved; they were rather of benign, degenerative, nature (**Graph 32**). On the other hand, a number of palaeopathological cases, particularly regarding those of endocranial wall changes, along with those of the ectocranial hyperporotic changes, and in combination with similar symptomatic manifestations on the appendicular structures, hence of systemic nature and/or coupled by the gravity of comorbidity issues, must have been quite serious, and with the probability to prove fatal; these were indicative of infectious conditions caused by pathogenicity of a range of causative agents including, but not limited, to aspects of zoonotic infectious-febrile diseases transmitted from domesticated animals and/or in relation to contamination of the dietary intake, i.e. from said animal byproducts, infection due to communicable diseases, and/or infectious complications secondary to trauma impact by external causes.

Trauma Manifestations

Cases of trauma impact were evaluated inspectionally[37] as an integral component of the palaeopathological analysis, having implemented a separate system of screening for the adequately preserved skeletal surfaces; one that discriminated against any deterioration, groove imprints, notches or similar indentation traces that may have been caused either taphonomically, by possible excavation trauma, curation handling, and/or by conditions in the museum repository environment. Hence, of the 55 individuals of the entire skeletal

---

[34] Including spondyloarthopathic changes on the occipital condyles.
[35] It should be further considered if the relation of eburnation manifestations affecting said subgroup may be indicative of *in vivo* specialization activities inclusive but not limited to occupational requirements.
[36] It is suggested that should preservation conditions issues have allowed it, there could have been additional palaeopathological manifestations documented among the 15 (27.27%) out of 55 individuals that could not be evaluated.
[37] As in all aspects of observational evaluations aided where relative by low stereoscopic magnification.

collection, 15 (27.27%) individuals showed inadequately preserved surfaces, whereas the remaining 40 (72.73%) were selected for analysis. Of the 40 individuals selected for study 30 (75.00%) showed an absence of discernible traces of trauma impact, whereas 10 (25.00%) individuals revealed traumatic manifestations[38]. **Graph 33** reflects said break down, based on the single versus the multiple interment group comparison with percentile values per subcategory, while the proportional prevalence between the two groups figure as follows. Among the 29 individuals of the single interment group with adequate skeletal preservation which were selected for trauma analysis, 20 (68.96%) showed absence of dental and skeletal trauma manifestations, whereas the remaining 9 homini (31.03%) scored positively. Amid the 11 individuals of the multiple interment group with adequate skeletal preservation for evaluations of trauma analysis only one individual showed trauma impact whereas the remaining 10 (90.90%) homini showed lack thereof. Regarding the documented manifestations of trauma impact, the proportional relations between the two groups revealed a prevalence of 31.03% among the individuals of the single interment group versus 9.09% amid those of the multiple interment group; hence the former exceeded in trauma prevalence the group of multiple interments by a 3.413 ratio.

The majority of the trauma impact sustained involved the postcranial skeleton, dominated by the axial structure of the vertebral column whereby there were four cases of Schmörl's nodes of a varied level of impact severity, ranging from moderate to severe[39], indicative of excessive load bearing stress or of accidental force afforded on the spine at nearly close approximation to axially, broadly supero-inferior, oriented directions. The four individuals involved were of male biological sex and ranged from "Middle to Late Adulthood" age subgroups, three of whom had been cremated. A "Middle Adult" individual of the latter subgroup, in addition to having sustained Schmörl's nodes, also presented a trace of trauma impact discerned by a clearly defined, sharply bordered, V-shaped outline along its length axis, having pierced a lumbar vertebral body up to the middle of its transversal width[40], indicative of an entry wound from the right dorsolateral surface toward a left ventro-lateral direction. Based on the anatomic locus of impact and the characteristic trace of the penetrating object which simulated the outline tip element of a spearhead, the puncture wound was diagnosed as of *perimortem* nature, caused by close encounter armed conflict, that had penetrated from the right dorsolateral region of the retroperitoneal anatomic space affording morbid wounds to venous and arterial vessels causing death primarily by excessive blood loss combined with organ failure.

In a sequence of diminishing prevalence of documented trauma conditions observed, there were two cases of Colle's fractures sustained by an older male and a female individual respectively, caused either by accidental fall, usually with an outstretched hand in dorsiflexion, or in a defensive posture to protect the neck and face by the raised forearm. Both cases had healed well, long before death, with discernible callus formations and in one of the two cases with a compromised radial articular realignment at the wrist joint.

Further, a case of dental trauma affected a left side deciduous first maxillary molar (m^1) of an individual (ca. 9 years of age) within the Infancy II age subgroup, due to excessive stress of masticatory causes, while three additional trauma cases affected adult individuals. These had included a healed rib fracture, traces of slight traumatic impact afforded on a humeral head, and a superficial cranial vault trauma. The latter was sustained by a young female, age assessed between 17-20 years. It pertained to a compressed fracture superiorly to the right frontal bone tuberosity (the locus of the frontal belly region of the right M. *occipitofrontalis* [M. *venter frontalis*]) that had been surgically treated, possibly to remove ectocranial bone splinters and to attend with a healing regimen, presenting a long before death well healed, smooth, ellipsoid outline with diameters measuring 8.97mm by 9.67mm, and 1.93mm in maximum depth.

---

[38] Comprising 18.18% out of the sample of 55 individuals.
[39] Such severe trauma impact was recorded among older individuals.
[40] Hence without an exit wound.

Non-Anthropological Organic Materials of Burial Contexts with Emphasis on Faunal Remains

Along with the anthropological remains, a considerable number of the burial contexts yielded samples of ecofactual materials of both inorganic and organic nature, some of which were components of the sedimentological attributes of the site's stratigraphic composition, while others, such as floral macro-components and soil fauna remnants (of the latter, some of the detritus chain), were indicative of the taphonomic environment characteristic of the human activity area's functional purpose. In addition, comprising a valuable component of burial contexts' cultural stratigraphic deposits were aggregates of faunal remains. These, being conterminal with the events of interring processes, presented a significant record of cultural data, which in addition to the value of their own zooarchaeological merit (Marean, Abe, Nilssen, and Stone 2001; Nicholson 1993; Spenneman and Colley 1989) could enable, based on the nature and specificity of their assemblages, the tracing of distinct funerary behaviors (Agelarakis 2011; Ahlberg 1971a; Garland 2001; Morris 1989; and 1992; Vermeule 1981) permanently bestowed by the ancients by the type and particular features of the animal bone fragments preserved, revealing important aspects of burial customs and of mortuary, sacrificial, practices.

Burial practices of funerary meals, the functional and symbolic provisioning of those at the threshold of Hades' gates during the interment event, as well as propitiating to the gods and deities of the underworld through ceremonial animal sacrifice were reflected, notwithstanding the passage of time, by the material evidence of the associated faunal remains; supporting the reasoning asserting clear reflections of awe, of dutiful respect and obligation for the burial and veneration of the dead, as well as of pious act, ritual, and religious conduct. Further, the considerable concentration of faunal remains representing sacrificial animals at this funerary activity area, and their inclusion as well as proximity to the human remains, signifies the importance of their function and of the blood ritual in the transitioning process to the afterlife.

A concise view of associations of the faunal materials and their distribution allocated by group of single or multiple interments is presented in **Graph 34**. Hence, faunal remains in dry and/or thermally altered form were associated with 28 (58.33%) out of the 48 burial contexts studied. Distribution aspects of preserved faunal remains documented among the groups of single versus the multiple interments revealed a 53.49% : 100% prevalence respectively; the latter exceeding the former by a ratio of 1.87.

The faunal remains associated with burial contexts were studied in a preliminary manner through the approaches of taphonomy and zooarchaeology. They offered evidence that illuminated processal conditions of sacrificial animal dressing, a roster of taxonomic classifications mainly to the genus level of the faunal assemblage represented, as well as the distribution of faunal anatomic components apportioned to the burial contexts juxtaposed to an assemblage of faunal remains recovered from an intra-site well context, functionally in use during the particular cultural component, suggested to have been mainly serving communal functions in the burial ground and/or of mortuary depository needs in relation to interment processes. The latter, is suggested, may offer an explanatory recommendation for 20 (46.51% out of 43) of the burial contexts of single interments (**Graph 34, and 35**) which were found during analysis void of a contextual association with faunal remains.

While it has been challenging, primarily due to issues of preservation, to discern accurate zoological taxonomic patterns across genus, size of individuals, and anatomical seriations from the assemblages of the faunal record associated with the burial contexts, continued research promises to better elucidate aspects of interest to zooarchaeology and the study of sacrificial offerings in funerary ritual at the site of *Plithos*. Nevertheless, faunal remains recovered in association within the burial contexts were compared to those recovered from the well context and it clearly appears that both revealed the taxonomic range of "expected" sacrificial animals in relation to funerary ritual and mortuary religious ceremony. This provided some insight into the complex and often regionally idiosyncratic facets of burial customs, reflecting on aspects of the human condition and the dynamics of the beliefs, obligations, and expectations in afterlife.

Hence, food animals dominated the profile of the faunal record whereby ovicaprical bones comprised the most prevalent aggregates, although a number of burial contexts yielded genera represented by a number of combinations between bovid[41], *Ovis, Capra, Sus*, and canid[42], as well as of several unidentified faunal individuals of smaller sizes. Eleven single interments involving cremated remains of male individuals[43] were found in association with both cremated and/or dry faunal remains in the following prevalence sequence. In eight of the eleven cases there were dry faunal remains, in two cases cremated remains, and in one case a combination of dry and cremated faunal remains. Further, in seven of the above cases the remains were of ovicaprical nature, and in the remaining four cases of suspected ovicaprical origin (**Graph 36**). Furthermore, along with the ovicaprical remains only two of those cases involved offerings of multiple genera, one with bovid remains and a second one with *Sus*.

Of the five contexts that involved multiple interments (**Graph 37**) there were four cases combining cremated and dry homini[44], involving dry faunal remains of ovicaprical nature, while the fifth case included ovicaprical bones along with a smaller in size unidentified faunal individual. Regarding, however, the twelve burial contexts which yielded single interments in dry form[45], the aggregates of associated faunal remains were found to exclusively be in dry form. Here, ten of the contexts included remains of ovicaprical nature, indiscriminately of biological age or age subgrouping, while in two of the contexts based on limited preservation of the faunal remains it was possible to only recon the presence of herbivoran[46] faunal remains. Individuals within the Infancy I and II cohorts were associated with dry ovicaprical remains without involvement of other identifiable genera; parenthetically as also observed with the four out of the five cases[47] of multiple interments where Infancy I and II individuals were involved, even though associated with mature in age male individuals. Thus it should be of interest to consider that in all cases of Infancy I and II individuals, in both single and multiple interments, there were associated ovicaprical remains, strictly of dry form. It appears that this correlation may not be coincidental, hence possibly reflecting on a pattern of the burial custom relative to the interment of young individuals; it appears that there had been no provisioning at their burial context with thermally altered/cremated sacrificial animal portions. Further with the individuals of the single interments group, although ovicaprical remains appear to have been the most prevalent of the domesticated animals to serve in the functions of the burial ritual, it was possible to discern that in five[48] (out of the seven) cases exclusively of female burial contexts, there had been offerings of multiple faunal genera. These involved two cases combining ovicaprical and *Sus* individuals, two cases with ovicaprical and bovid individuals, and one case that combined ovicaprical, *Sus*, and bovid individuals. It thus appears that these post-subadult in age female interments retained an association with the richest record of faunal offerings/provisioning among the entire membership of the population sample recovered at *Plithos*, particularly compared with the rest of the post-subadulthood individuals involved.

Overall, the faunal record offered additional, valuable, diagnostic traces of human activity through the traces of mechanical impacts sustained on bone surfaces. There were sixty cases of both superficial and deeper animal dressing cut marks documented on the osseous surfaces, as well as through and through

---

[41] Suggested of domesticated cattle, of genus *Bos*.
[42] Of the taxonomic family of *Canidae*.
[43] Age subgroup distribution using the abbreviations of Graph 11: 1 YA; 1 YAMA; 2 MA; 1 MALA; 2 LA; and 4 GA.
[44] Relative burial contexts with homini, age and where possible biological sex assessments: 1) dry remains of 1 MALA male and 1 IN II individual; 2) dry remains of 1MALA probable male and 1 IN I individual; 3) 1 GA male and 1 IN I individual; and 4) 3 cremated males (1 MA, and 2 GA) and dry remains of an 1 IN I individual.
[45] Age and where possible biological sex subgroupings: 2 IN I; 1 in later IN II (possibly female); 2 YAMA (1 female and 1 probable male); 3 MA females; and 4 GA (3 females and 1 probable male).
[46] Taxonomic class *Mammalia*.
[47] The fifth case included the remains of a cremated YA male, and the dry remains of a GA female, associated with cremated and dry in form ovicaprical remains, along with the remains of an unidentified, small in size, faunal individual.
[48] Age subgroups: 1 YAMA; 2 MA, and 2 GA.

cuts[49] in apportioning edible shares and as importantly of non-edible but of symbolically important components of the faunal anatomical parts, apparently as mandated by the burial customs and practice. In reference to horn cores, out of the several cases identified only once was there an association with a female individual,[50] from the single interment group. Hence, the vast majority of horn core remains were associated with male individuals.

In aiming to address the cluster of the 20 single interment contexts that were found not to have been associated with faunal remains, they comprised 46.51% out of the group of 43 single interments involving an isometric distribution of ten inhumations and ten cremations. In aiming to provide an explanation for the absence of faunal remains, potentially as part of the burial custom, it was considered that the possibility could not be excluded whereby faunal offerings could had been deposited in other site relative contexts, as for example alluded above referring to the well feature that had served as a repository context for relevant functions of the funerary rights. Further, regarding particularly the cremations involved, the offerings of faunal materials, could have been allocated to contiguous contexts used during the procedure of the burial custom at the juncture when the interment was under pyre exposure. Overall, in relation to the demographic composition, the individuals from the 20 burial contexts appeared to lack any patterns of discrimination against age or biological sex subgroups; both biological sex subgroupings and all age cohorts were involved. This was in concert with the distribution dynamics of biological sex and age cohorts documented among the rest of the population sample that had been associated with remains of faunal offerings. Hence there were no discernible patterns of varied analogy on those parameters between these two population groups that could for example provide clues on different mortality causing circumstances, such as the strike of an epidemic that could have necessitated a hurried implementation of the burial rights, nor were there any discernible archaeological anthropology cues retrieved that would have reflected on a perfunctory act of interment process. Further, looking into the possibility of skeletal biological growth and physiology issues, along with morphological observations on skeletal robustness, and of the prevalence and specificity of MHOS changes, there was no percipient variability that could be established between those individuals associated with remains of faunal offerings, versus those without them. A distinct correlation was made notable among the individuals lacking association with remains of faunal offerings, from the domain of palaeopathology. Seven (out of ten) of the inhumed individuals that had retained cranial vault bones showed manifestations of hyperporotic changes[51]. Such a prevalence of palaeopathologic manifestations however was not established among the subset of cremated individuals lacking association with offerings of faunal remains, while the particular palaeopathologic manifestation was not absent from the population group that was associated with faunal remains.

It thus appears that the only perceptible distinction characterizing the 20 burial contexts lacking tangible association with offerings of faunal remains, as afforded through the bioarchaeological study[52] of the osseous record, laid in the fact that they comprised a subset (46.51% out of 43) of the single interments' group. If the possibilities alluded above such as that the well feature or adjoining contexts may have served a relative repository function, and/or even if any taphonomic in nature causative agent(s) could not offer a plausible explanation, the anthropological analysis void of data contributed from the study of the archaeological record, could not lend support to an explanatory hypothesis arguing for differences in the domain age, biological sex or socio-economic standing. Regarding the burial custom of inhumation and cremation, both were practiced as with the rest of the population sample. Regarding a concise osteological point of view there appeared to have been no clearly defined distinctions as far as variability in skeletal biologic growth and development compared to the rest of the population sample. Similarly, there were no

---

[49] There were transversal cuts on the long axes of appendiculat skeleton fore-, and hind limbs particularly of larger faunal individuals, while horn cores of both ovis and capra attested to cuts of similar direction.
[50] This case included the ovicaprical horn core and *Sus* remains.
[51] Hence a 100% observation ratio.
[52] Without tangible results of high technology archaeometric-molecular studies.

differences in the preparation quality of dietary intake[53] and in the rostrum of dental pathologies sustained. There were no apparent dissimilarities in skeletal physiology and skeletomuscular changes. The overall palaeopathogic profile offered no sharp differences from early life stressors, to communicable diseases, and degenerative conditions. Further there were no distinctions on aspects of the demographic dynamics.

Epilogue

While the project involving the bioarchaeological study of the 55 human skeletal individuals, see Graph 2, and where available of the zooarchaeological record, recovered at the *Plithos* formal burial ground in *Chora* of Naxos island is ongoing, a number of demographic and palaeopathological dynamics may reflect on aspects of the human condition and funerary customs during the Geometric period. Both burial processes of cremation (**Table 5**), and inhumation had been practiced, see Graph 3. It appears that the burial custom of cremations was distinctly performed according to biological sex and age subgrouping restricted to male individuals from the later years of "SubAdulthood" to terminal "Late Adulthood"; apparently according to additional cultural filters observed as there were individuals within the male cluster from late "SubAdulthood" through the range of the adulthood cohorts that excluded from this funerary practice had been inhumed. Apropos, it should be noted that the record of cremated bone remains revealed the only case of deep penetrating, *splanchnic* and *perimortem*, trauma impact that had been caused by armed conflict. Although in matters of statistical implications this is considered as evidence of circumstantial nature, qualitative evidence is provided nevertheless that ties mortality due to armed conflict with the funerary right of cremation.

The population sample included *homini* that had been buried as single (43), and multiple (12) interments in 48 burial contexts. The group of multiple interments comprised 7 inhumations and 5 cremations in mostly combining infants with adult males, indicative of a funerary practice that did not mandate the interring of very young individuals in a spatially separate burial ground or a specific, dedicated, allocation within the funerary domain of the adults' cemetery. Regarding the 43 graves with single interments a nearly equal distribution was identified between 22 inhumed and 21 cremated individuals. Apropos, at an inter-site comparative context similar conditions were documented at the Geometric burial ground at *Pythagoreion* of Samos island (Agelarakis, 2003).

On matters of biological growth and bone plasticity changes, the anatomic morphology of the population sample showed with a relative range of variability along biological sex differentiation well-built skeletal bodies, indicative of robust developmental growth during the maturation processes, and lacking significant emphasis of discernible, seriously impairing early life stressors caused by physical or social environmental parameters. Particularly, skeleto-anatomic manifestations in relation to kinetics indicated that age subgroups of both male and female individuals, from the later years of "Subadulthood" (16-17y.) to terminal "Middle Adulthood" (at ca. 45 y.) had been actively involved in demanding physical activities including, but not limited to, those related to food production and economic output processes such as those in agriculture and/or in maritime activities.

Further, on matters of demographic dynamics, an abridged distribution of biological sex assessments indicated that the cluster of 31 male individuals comprised 56.36%, the female cluster of 14 individuals 25.45%, and the subgroup of "Indeterminate" 18.18% of the population sample (see Graph 10). Regarding the mortality prevalence, it clearly appears that the combined "Infancy" age subgroups reflected on life periods with tumultuous health episodes (suggested to have been the result of a combination of weanling conditions, childhood infectious diseases, and comorbidity) for the survivorship of those young age subgroups; the demographic attrition curve reaching at that cohort a tally of 18.17% (**Graph 38**). Subsequently the mortality score among the "Subadults" remained isometric as during the "Infancy II" subgroup, at 7.27%, indicative of a cautiously safer period for the prospects of survivorship for the

---

[53] Through the domain of dental anthropology.

membership of these cohorts than "Infancy I", whereas attrition effects clearly tripled among the "Young Adults" at 22.10%, crested at the apex of 28.47% among the "Middle Adults", and subsequently declined at 21.20% within the years of the "Late Adults"; the combined adulthood cohorts comprised an ominous 71.78% of the population attrition record. Successively it sharply tapered off at a level of insignificant score values among the cohorts of "*Maturus*" and the "Older"; illuminating as it may be of the rather unfavorable expectations faced by the grizzling members of this population sample for longevity-probability past the *terminus* of the "Late Adulthood", after approximately the 45th year of age.

Apropos to the demographic components of mortality and survivorship reflected by the population sample of the site, a juxtaposition to comparable data from the burial ground at *Pythagoreion* of Samos island may provide facets of the elemental dynamics that were in effect at the background milieu; and had ingrained the mode of experiences and realities at an inter-site environment during the Geometric period (**Graphs 38, and 39**). It appears, based on proportional scores, that at *Pythagoreion* of Samos, population attrition uniquely initiated during the critical "Perinatal"[54] period, a mortality element absent from *Plithos* of Naxos, coupled by the fact that *Plithos* faired a fourfold better in survivorship during "Infancy I" than at *Pythagoreion* where mortality at said age cohort reached a sinister 42.58% (**Graph 40**). Should the palaeopathologist lump the mortality scores of "Perinatal" and "Infancy I" at *Pythagoreion*, it would reach an ominous score of 50.39%. In the subsequent age subgroups however, between "Infancy II" through to "Late Adults" *Plithos* exceeded *Pythagoreion* in mortality, notably surpassing the Samians at *Pythagoreion* with a mortality apex of more than a sixth fold prevalence within the "SubAdulthood" age subgroup, indicative of taxing conditions that had been in effect during this age cohort at *Plithos*. Although not as sharply, *Plithos* continued the trend to exceed *Pythagoreion* in the mortality prevalence of its membership within the three sequent age subgroups of adulthood. *Plithos* slightly yielded in demographic attrition prevalence to *Pythagoreion* during the "*Maturus*" years. Yet in retrospect, this was to reveal of the diminished longevity probabilities of "Late Adults" at *Plithos* to reach old age.

Naxos island, with its pivotal geolocation within the Cyclades, the splendor of its natural beauty, its landscape magnificence and catchment area, was bound nevertheless to present limitations in available resources to adequately provide for the increasing needs, ambitions, and growth prospects of a largely agriculturally based and yet actively seafaring-supported society. Unavoidably, Naxos was to be involved with competitive and challenging antagonists, best exemplified in its relations with its most proximal of its neighboring islands, namely Paros[55], on matters of strategic political and military alliances[56], resource acquisition, the strive for power in maritime routes, and in endeavors seeking to establish and secure other important seaworthy locations in the Aegean Archipelago and the Eastern Mediterranean for trade and settlement.

It is hoped that the study of the human skeletal population sample from the *Plithos* burial ground may offer tesserae of testimony from Naxos, allowing to bear witness in retrospect even if only of a select number of essentials on conditions that both determined and oversaw life events during the Geometric period.

Continued research on the wealth of information that can be retrieved from the human and zooarchaeological skeletal records promises to yield additional clues, in conjunction with the rest of the archaeological record, in deciphering additional features of the human condition during this period which formed the realities and expectations of the Archaic Period at the pivotal Cycladic region in the sea routes of southeastern Europe, western Asia, and northern Africa.

---

[54] An age subgroup defined by the period around the time of birth (slightly before to slightly after birth).
[55] A decisive victory of the Parians against the Naxians is described in Greek Iambic Poetry: *Archilochus*, Testimonia, no 4 (*Sosthenis inscriptio*), A Col. Ia. 50-55, p. 30. For the death of Parian poet Archilochus, in armed conflict, by the Naxian *Callondes* cf. *Plutarch*, Moralia, Περί των υπό του θείου βραδέως τιμωρουμένων 560.
[56] In reference to the Lelantine War, cf. *Herodotus*, 5.99; *Plutarch*, Moralia, Ερωτικός 760-761; *Plutarch*, Moralia, Των επτά σοφών συμπόσιον 153f; The latter reference is further cross-substantiated by *Hesiod* who refers in his Works and Days, v. 654-657, to the poetic competition he won in honor of Chalkidian Amphidamas who fell in the Lelantine battles fighting the Eretrians, cf. Athanassakis 2004, commentary 654-659, p:103.

References Cited

Agelarakis, P. A., (1996) A Field and Laboratory Manual for Archaeologists, for the Excavation, Documentation, and Preservation of Human Osseous Remains. *Ariadne*, 8, 189-247;

Agelarakis, P. A., (1996a) The Archaeology of Human Bones: Prehistoric Copper Producing Peoples in the Khao Wong Prachan Valley, Central Thailand. In (ed.) P. Bellwood. The Indo-Pacific Prehistory: The Chang Mai Papers, IPAA Bulletin 14:1, 133-139.

Agelarakis, P. A., (2003). Preliminary Anthropology Database Report-Pythagoreion of Samos, Archival, KA' Ephoreia of Prehistoric and Classical Antiquities; Final Anthropology Report in preparation.

Agelarakis, P. A., (2005) The Anthropology of Tomb A1K1 of Orthi Petra in Eleutherna. A Narrative of the Bones: Aspects of the Human Condition in Geometric-Archaic Eleutherna. University of Crete, Rethymnon.

Agelarakis, P. A., (2011) A Dignified Passage through the Gates of Hades: The Burial Custom of Cremations at Orthi Petra in Eleutherna, Rethymno-Crete, Greece, Abstracts, 11th International Cretological Congress, 21-27/10/2011, Rethymnon, 264-265.

Agelarakis, P. A., (2013) On the Anthropology Project of 35 Salaminos Street Site of Kerameikos, Athens: A Brief Account. Archaeologikés Symvolés, Volume B: Attika, A' and Γ' Prehistoric and Classical Antiquities Authorities, Museum of Cycladic Art, Athens, 369-386.

Agelarakis, P. A., (2014) On the Preservation and Conservation of Archaeologically Recovered Anthropological Remains: A Brief Communication to Younger Colleagues. In (ed.) E. Korka The Protection of Archaeological Heritage in Times of Economic Crisis, Cambridge Scholars Publishing, Newcastle upon Tyne, 254-259.

Ahlberg, G., (1971). Fighting on Land and Sea in Greek Geometric Art. Stockholm, 1971.

Ahlberg, G., (1971a) Prothesis and Ekphora in Greek Geometric Art. Göteborg.

Angel, J. L., (1981). History and development of paleopathology. American Journal in Physical Anthropology 56, 509-515.

Athanassakis, N.A., (2004). Hesiod: Theogony, Works and Days, Shield (2nd ed.). The John Hopkins University Press, Baltimore.

Aufderheide, C.A., and Rodriguez-Martin, C., Langsjoen, O., (1998). The Cambridge Encyclopedia of Human Paleopathology. Cambridge University Press, Cambridge.

Bass, M.W., (2005). Human Osteology: A Laboratory and Field Manual, (5th ed.). Missouri Archaeological Society, Special Publication 2, Columbia.

Boardman, J., (1998). Early Greek Vase Painting: 11th -6th Centuries BC. Thames and Hudson, London.

Bohnert, M., Rost, T., Pollak, S., (1998). The degree of destruction of human bodies in relation to the duration of the fire. Forensic Sci. Int. 95, 11-21.

Brothwell, D.R., (1981). Digging up Bones: The excavation treatment and study of human skeletal remains. Ithaca: Cornell University Press.

Buikstra, J.E., and Beck, L.A., (2006). (Eds.). Bioarchaeology: The contextual analysis of human remains. Elsevier, New York.

Buikstra, J.E., Swegle, M., (1989). Bone modification due to burning: experimental evidence. In: Bonnichsen, R.B., Sorg, M.H. (Eds.), Bone Modification Center for the Study of the First Americans. Orono, MN, 258-278.

Chochol, J., (1961). Anthropologische Analyse menschlicher Brandreste aus den Lausitzer Gräberfeldern in Usti Nad Labem-Strekov II und in Zirovice, Bezirk Cheb. In: Plesl, E. (Ed.), Die Lausitzer Kultur in Nordwestbohmen. (Monumenta Archaeologica 8), Akademie der Wissenschaften, Prag, 273-290.

Coldstream, J.N., (2003). Geometric Greece. Routledge, New York.

Devlin, J.B., Herrmann, N.P., (2015). Bone color as an interpretive tool of the depositional history of archaeological cremains. The Analysis of Burned Human Remains, Elsevier, Amsterdam.

Garland, R., (2001). The Greek Way of Death. Cornell University Press, Ithaca.

Gejvall, N.G., (1963). Cremations. In: Brothwell, D., Higgs, E. (Eds.), Science in Archaeology. Thames and Hudson, London, 468-479.

Gejvall, N.G., (1969). Cremations. In: Brothwell, D., Higgs, E. (Eds.), Science in Archaeology Praeger, New York, 468-479.

Graw, M., Wahl, J., Ahlbrecht, M., (2005). Course of the meatus acusticus internus as criterion for sex

differentiation. Forensic Sci. Int. 147, 113-117.
Greek Iambic Poetry: Archilochus, Testimonia, no 4 (*Sosthenis inscriptio*), A Col. Ia. 50-55, p. 30.
Haglund, W.D., Sorg, M.H., (1997). Introduction to forensic taphonomy. In: Haglund, W.D., Sorg, M.H. (Eds.), Forensic Taphonomy: The Postmortem Fate of Human Remains. CRC Press, Boca Raton, 1-9.
Herodotus, (1953). Ιστορία. Α. Θεοφίλου, Πάπυρος, Αθήνα, Ε' (5), 99, 323.
Hesiod, (2006). Works and Days. (Eds.) J. Henderson, and G.W. Most (Translator), LCL, 57, 86-153.
Hillson S., 2002. Dental Anthropology. Cambridge University Press, New York.
Jankauskas, R., Barakauskas, S., Bojarun, R., (2001). Incremental lines of dental cementum in biological age estimation. Homo 52, 59-71.
Iscan, M.Y., and Kennedy, K.A.R. (1989). (Eds.): Reconstruction of life from the skeleton. Alan R. Liss, New York.
Kirk, S. G., (1949). Ships on Geometric Vases. The British School at Athens, Annual 44, 93-153.
Komar, A.D., and Buikstra, E.J., (2008). Forensic Anthropology: Contemporary Theory and Practice. Oxford University Press, New York.
Kourou, N., (1984). Local Naxian Workshops andt he Import-Export Pottery Trade of the Island in the Geometric Period. In (Ed.) H.A.G.Brijder, Ancient Greek and Related Pottery. Proceedings of the International Vase Symposium in Amsterdam, Amsterdam, 107-112.
Kourou, N., (1998). Euboea and Naxos in the Late Geometric Period: The Cesnola Style. In (Eds.) M. Bats and B. D'Agostino (éds.), Euboica. L' Eubea e le presenza euboica in Calcidica e in Occidente. Atti del convegno interna-zionale di Napoli, Napoli, 167-177.
Kourou, N., (1999). Ανασκαφές Νάξου. Το Νότιο Νεκροταφείο της Νάξου κατά τη Γεωμετρική Περίοδο, Athens.
Krogman, W. M., and Iscan, M.Y., (1986). The human skeleton in forensic medicine (2nd ed.). C. C. Thomas, Springfield.
Lambrinoudakis, V.K., (1988). Veneration of Ancestors in Geometric Naxos. In (Eds.) R. Hägg, N. Marinatos, and G.C. Nordquist, Early Greek Cult Practice. Proceedings of the Third International Symposium at the Swedish Institute in Athens, Stockholm, 235-246.
Larsen, C. S., (1997). Bioarchaeology: Interpreting behavior from the human skeleton. Cambridge University Press, London.
Malinowski, A., Porawski, R., 1969. Identifikationsmöglichkeiten menschlicher Brand-knochen mit besonderer Berücksichtigung ihres Gewichts. Zacchia 44, 1-19
Marean, C., Abe, Y., Nilssen, P., Stone, E., (2001). Estimating the minimum number of skeletal elements (MNE) in zooarchaeology: a review and a new image-analysis GIS approach. Am. Antiq. 66, 333-348.
Moore, M., B., (2000). Ships on a 'Wine-Dark Sea' in the Age of Homer. Metropolitan Museum Journal, 35, 13-38.
Morris, I., (1989). Burial and Ancient Society: The Rise of the Greek City-State. Cambridge University Press, London.
Morris, I., (1992). Death-Ritual and Social Structure in Classical Antiquity.Cambridge University Press, New York.
Morrison, S. J., and Williams, T. R., (1968). Greek Oared Ships: 900-322 B.C., Cambridge.
Muller, M., Berytrand, M.F., Quatrehomme, G., M. Bolla, and J. P. Rocca, (1998). Macroscopic and microscopic aspects of incinerated teeth. J. Forensic Odontostomatol. 16, 1-7.
Munsell Color Company, (2000). Munsell Soil Color Charts. Munsell Color GretagMacbeth, New Windsor, NY.
Myers, S.L., Williams, J.M., Hodges, J.S., (1999). Effects of extreme heat on teeth with implications for histologic processing. J. Forensic Sci. 44, 805-809.
Nicholson, R., (1993). A morphological investigation of burnt animal bone and an evaluation of its utility in archaeology. J. Archaeol. Sci. 20, 411-428.
Norén, A., Lynnerup, N., Czarnetzki, A., Graw, M., (2005). Lateral angle: A method for sexing using the petrous bone. Am. J. Phys. Anthropol. 128, 318-323.
Ortner, J. D., (2003). Identification of pathological conditions in human skeletal remains. Smithsonian Institution Press, Washington, D.C.
Ortner, J. D., Putschard, J.C. W., (1981). Identification of pathological Conditions in Human Skeletal Remains. Reprint Edition of Smithsonian Contributions to Anthropology, Number 28. Smithsonian Institution Press, Washington.

Plutarch, Moralia, Περὶ τῶν ὑπὸ τοῦ θείου βραδέως τιμωρουμένων 560.
Plutarch, Moralia, Ἐρωτικός 760-761.
Plutarch, Moralia, Τῶν ἑπτὰ σοφῶν συμπόσιον 153f.
Pusch, C., Broghammer, M., Scholz, M., (2000). Cremation practices and the survival of ancient DNA: burnt bone analyses via RAPD-mediated PCR. Anthrop. Anz. 58, 237-251.
Reber, K., (2011). Céramique eubéenne à Naxos au début de l' Âge du Fer. In (Ed.) A. Mazarakis, The "Dark Ages" Revisited. Acts of an international symposium in memory of William D.E. Coulson, Volos, 929-942.
Reber, K., and Zapheiropoulou, P., (2012). Plithos on Naxos. An Early Iron Age Cemetery. Zagora in Context, Settlements and Intercommunal Links in the Geometric Period (900-700 BC), Meditarch. 25, Abstracts, 317.
Shipman, P., Foster, G., Schoeninger, M., (1984). Burnt bones and teeth: an experimental study of color, morphology, crystal structure and shrinkage. J. Archaeol. Sci. 11, 307-325.
Shipman, P., Walker, A., and Bichell, D., (1985). The human skeleton. Harvard Press, Cambridge.
Snodgrass, M.A., (2000). The Dark Age of Greece. Routledge, New York.
Spenneman, D., Colley, S., (1989). Fire in a pit: the effects of burning on faunal remains. Archaeozoologia 3, 51-64.
Steele, D. G., and Bramblett, C. A., (1988). The anatomy and biology of the human skeleton. Texas A&M University Press, College Station.
Schweitzer, B., (1971). Greek Geometric Art. Phaidon, New York.
Thompson, T.J.U., (2004). Recent advances in the study of burned bone and their implications for forensic anthropology. Forensic Sci. Int. 146S, 203-205.
Thompson, T.J.U., (2005). Heat-induced dimensional changes in bone and their consequences for forensic anthropology. J. Forensic Sci. 50 (5), 1008-1015.
Ubelaker, D. H., (1982). The development of American paleopathology. In Spencer, F. (Ed.): A History of American Physical Anthropology 1930-1980. Academic Press, New York.
Ubelaker, D.H., (1999). Human Skeletal Remains: Excavation, Analysis, Interpretation. Washington, Taraxacum, DC.
van Vark, G.N., (1974). The investigation of human cremated skeletal material by multivariate statistical methods. I. Methodology. Ossa 1, 63-95.
van Vark, G.N., (1975). The investigation of human cremated skeletal material by multivariate statistical methods. II. Measures. Ossa 2, 47-53.
Vermeule, E., (1981). Aspects of Death in Early Greek Art and Poetry. University of California Press, Berkeley.
Wahl, J., (1983). A contribution to metrical age determination of cremated subadults. Homo 34, 48-54.
Wells, C., (1960). The study of cremation. Antiquity 34, 29-37.
White, T.D., and Folkens, P.A., (1991). Human Osteology. New York, Academic Press.
Zafeiropoulou F., and Agelarakis A., (2005), "Warriors of Paros", Archaeology 58, 1, 30 - 35.
Zafeiropoulou, F., (2007). Νέα στοιχεία για την γεωμετρική Ναξο. Το νεκροταφείο στη θέση Πλίθος της Χώρας. Abstracts, The «Dark Ages» Revisited. An International Conference in Memory of William D.E. Coulson, Volos.
Zapheiropoulou, P., (1983). Γεωμετρικά Αγγεία από τη Νάξο, ASAtene 45, 121-136.
Zapheiropoulou, P., (1988). Naxos: Monuments and Museum, Athens.
Zapheiropoulou, P., (2001). Καύσεις στις Γεωμετρικές Κυκλάδες: Οι Περιπτώσεις της Νάξου και της Πάρου. In (Ed.) N.Ch. Stampolidis, Καύσεις στην Εποχή του Χαλκού και την Πρώϊμη Εποχή του Σιδήρου, Athens, 285-299.
Zapheiropoulou, P., (2003). La necropoli geometrica di Tsikalario a Naxos, Magna Graecia, 18, 5-6.

Acknowledgements

The author thanks Argie Agelarakis, MA, for serving as project crew chief during the field seasons in Paroikia-Paros Island. The front and back covers of this publication are hers, inspired by the midsummer etesian winds' interplay with the Aegean waves. Thanks are also extended to Dr. F. Zapheiropoulou, Ephor of Antiquities Emerita and site excavator, for inviting me to study the anthropological materials. Further, the author thanks his student assistants who worked in the field, in Naxos, and at the lab at Adelphi University, A. Sardis, G. and A. Dovas, D. Schoenfuss, S. Zawistowski, A. Adler, K. Lombardy, P. Agelarakis, and L. Jacobsen.

Graphs

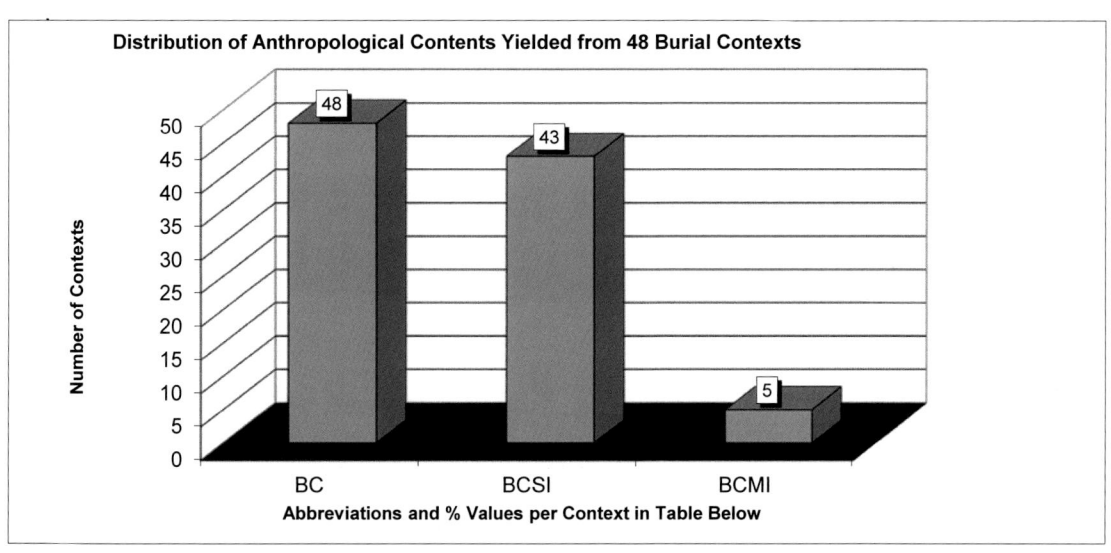

Graph Abbreviations		% Values per Category
BC	= Burial Contexts (48)	100.00%
BCSI	= Contexts with Single Interments (43)	89.59%
BCMI	= Contexts with Multiple Interments (5)	10.41%

GRAPH 1

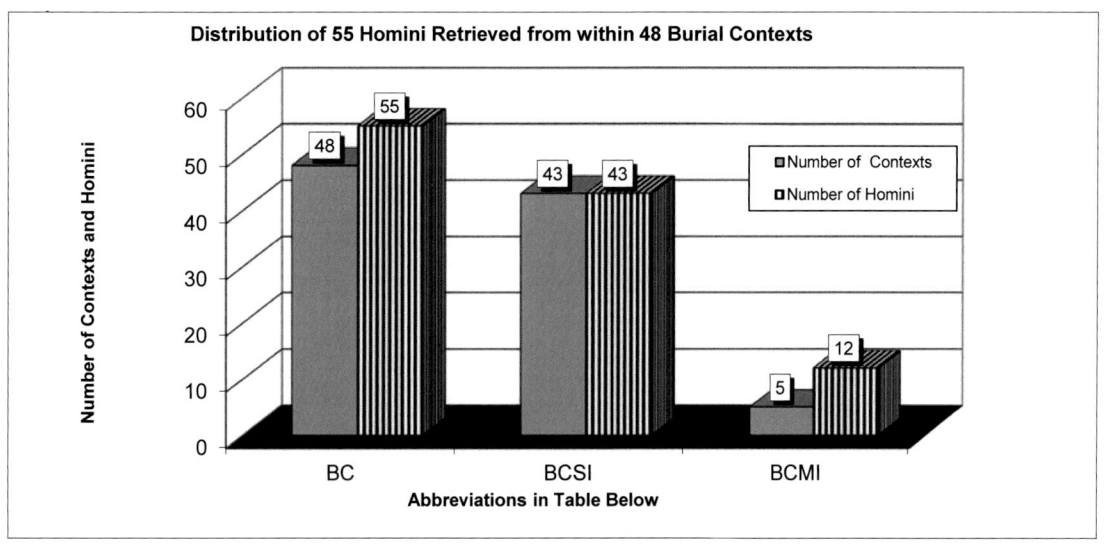

Graph Abbreviations	
BC	= Total of 48 Burial Contexts which Yielded 55 Homini
BCSI	= 43 Burial Contexts with Single Interments which Yielded 43 Homini
BCMI	= 5 Burial Contexts with Multiple Interments which Yielded 12 Homini

GRAPH 2

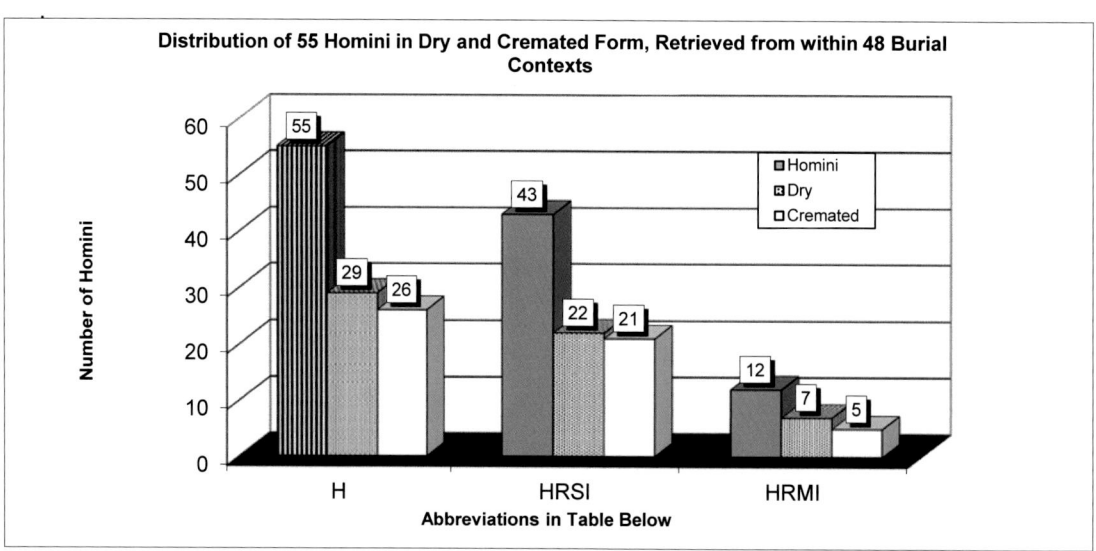

GRAPH 3

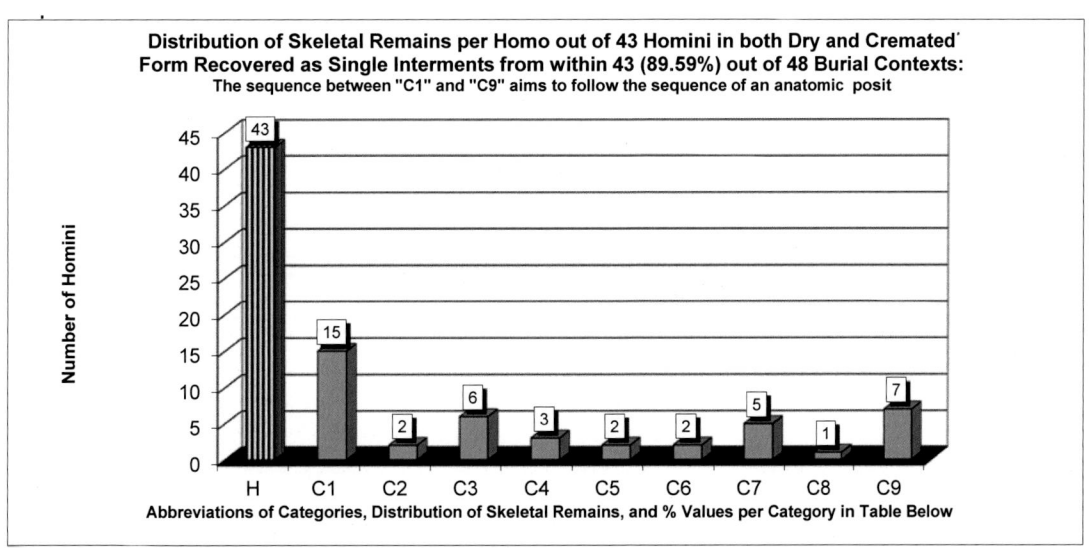

		Graph Abbreviations		% Values per Category out of 43 Homini
H	=	43 Single Interments, 22 in Dry, and 21 in Cremated Form	=	100.00%
C1	=	Homini represented by Cranial, Dental, Postcranial Axial, and Appendicular remains (15)	=	34.88%
C2	=	Homini represented by Cranial, Dental, and Postcranial Appendicular remains (2)	=	4.65%
C3	=	Homini represented by Cranial, Postcranial Axial, and Appendicular remains (6)	=	13.95%
C4	=	Homini represented by Cranial and Postcranial Appendicular remains (3)	=	6.98%
C5	=	Homini represented by Cranial, Dental, and Postcranial Axial remains (2)	=	4.65%
C6	=	Homini represented by Cranial and Dental remains (2)	=	4.65%
C7	=	Homini represented by Cranial remains (5)	=	11.62%
C8	=	Homini represented by Postcranial Axial and Appendicular remains (1)	=	2.32%
C9	=	Homini represented by Postcranial Appendicular remains (7)	=	16.27%

GRAPH 4

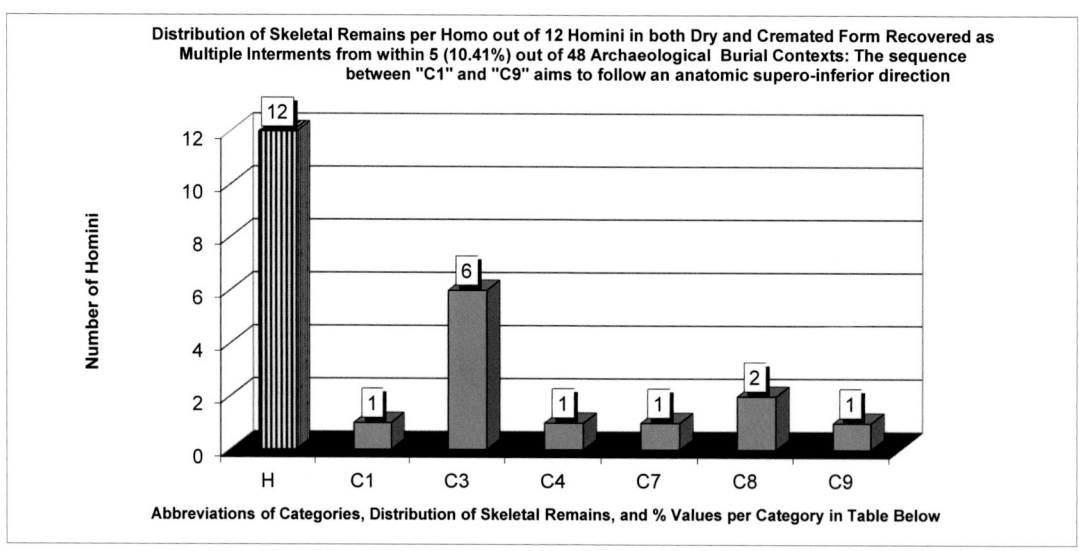

GRAPH 5

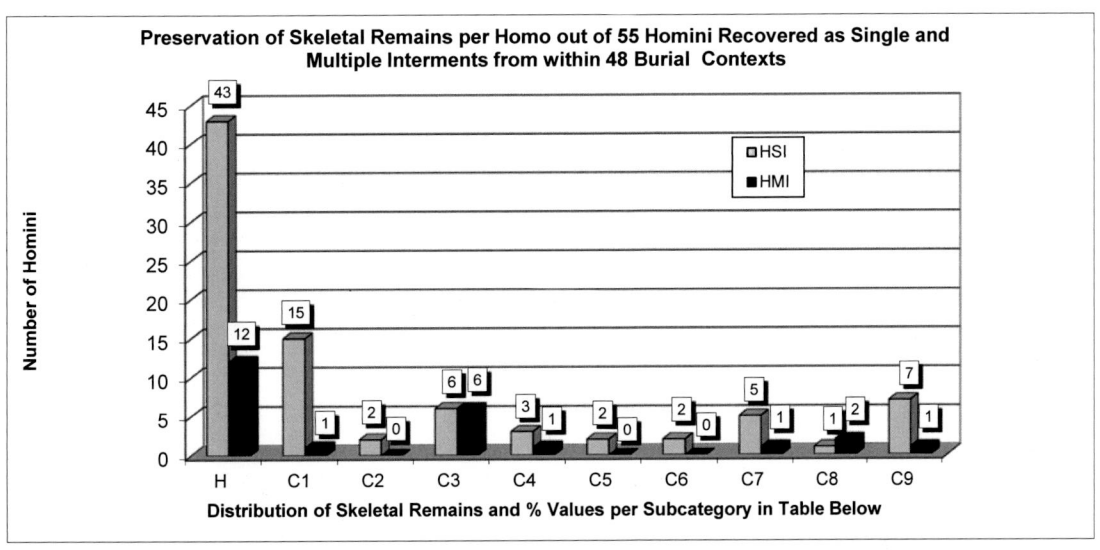

	Graph Abbreviations, and Values per subcategory	
H	=	55 Homini Recovered as Single (43 or 78.18%), and Multiple Interments (12 or 21.81%)
C1	=	16 (29.09%) out of 55 Homini which Yielded Cranial, Dental, Postcranial Axial, and Appendicular Remains as Single (15 or 93.75% out of 16) and Multiple (1 or 6.25% out of 16) Interments
C2	=	2 (3.63%) out of 55 Homini as Single Interments which Yielded Cranial, Dental, and Postcranial Appendicular Remains
C3	=	12 (21.81%) out of 55 Homini which Yielded Cranial, Postcranial Axial, and Appendicular Remains as Single (6 or 50.0% out of 12) and Multiple (6 or 50.0% out of 12) Interments
C4	=	4 (7.27%) out of 55 Homini which Yielded Cranial and Postcranial Appendicular Remains as Single (3 or 75.00% out of 4) and multiple (1 or 25.00% out of 4) Interments
C5	=	2 (3.63%) out of 55 Homini which Yielded Cranial, Dental, and Postcranial Axial Remains as Single Interments
C6	=	2 (3.63%) out of 55 Homini which Yielded Cranial and Dental Remains as Single Interments
C7	=	6 (10.90%) out of 55 Homini which Yielded Cranial Remains as Single (5 or 83.33% out of 6) and Multiple (1 or 16.66% out of 6) Interments
C8	=	3 (5.45%) out of 55 Homini which Yielded Postcranial Axial and Appendicular Remains as Single (1 or 33.33 % out of 3) and Multiple (2 or 66.66% out of 3) Interments
C9	=	8 (14.54%) out of 55 Homini which Yielded Postcranial Appendicular Remains as Single (7 or 87.5% out of 8) and Multiple (1 or 12.5% out of 8) Interments

GRAPH 6

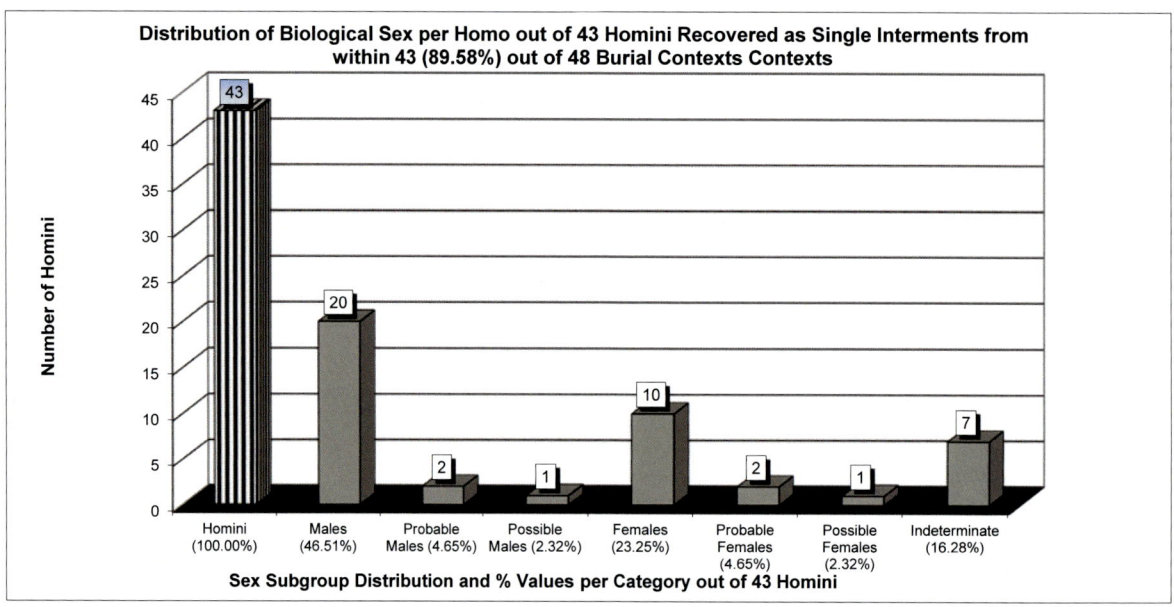

GRAPH 7

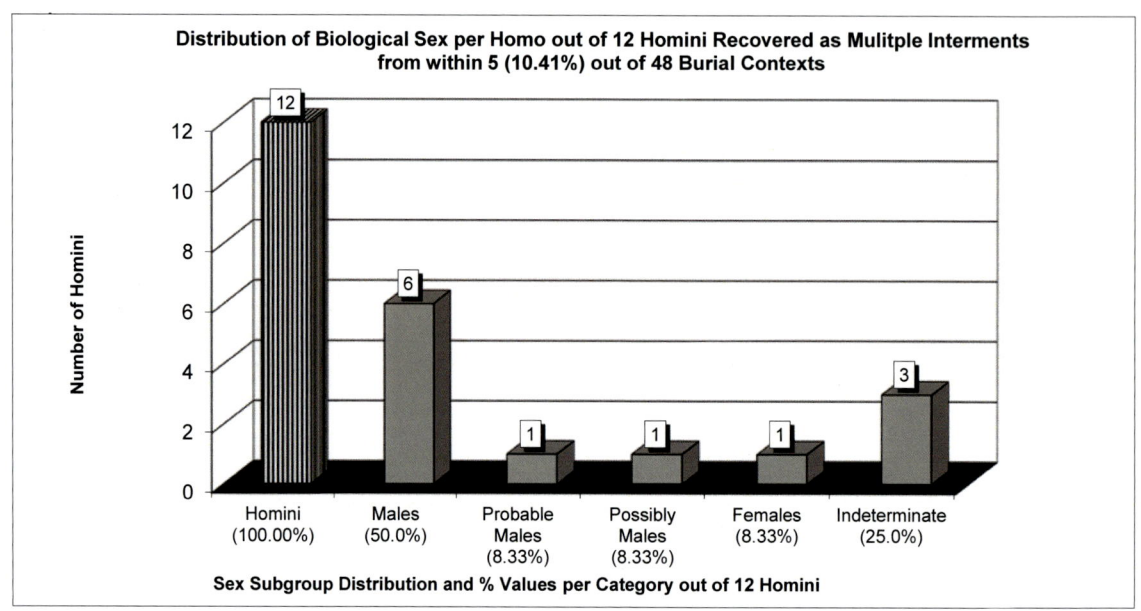

GRAPH 8

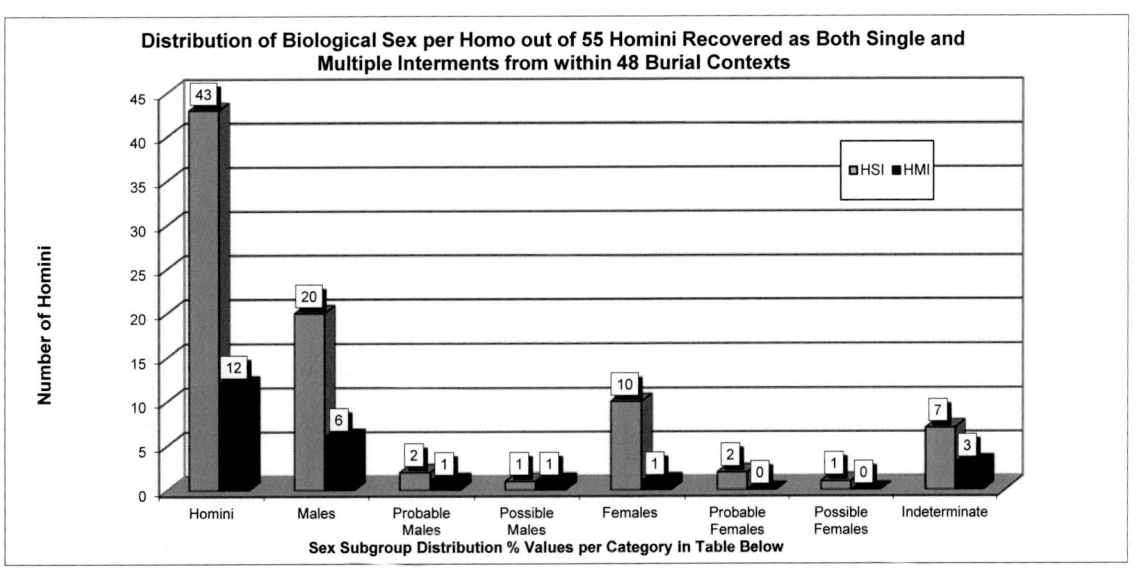

		Graph Abbreviations, and Values per Subcategory
Homini	=	55 Homini Recovered as Single (43 or 78.18% out of 55) and Multiple Interments (12 or 21.81% out of 55) from 48 Burial Contexts
Males	=	26 (47.27% out of 55) Homini Determined to be Male, Recovered as Single (20 or 76.92% out of 26), and Multiple (6 or 23.07% out of 26) Interments
Probable Males	=	3 (5.45% out of 55) Homini Determined to be Probable Males, Recovered as Single (2 or 66.66% out of 3), and Multiple (1 or 33.33% out of 3) Interments
Possible Males	=	2 (3.63% out of 55) Homini Determined to be Possible Males, Recovered as Single (1 or 50.0% out of 2), and Multiple (1 or 50.0% out of 2) Interments
Females	=	11 (20.0% out of 55) Homini Determined to be Female, Recovered as Single (10 or 90.90% out of 11), and Multiple (1 or 9.09% out of 11) Interments
Probable Females	=	2 (3.63% out of 55) homini determined to be Probable Females recovered as single interments
Possible Females		1 (1.82% out of 55) Homo Determined to be a Possible Female, Recovered as a Single Interment
Indeterminate	=	10 (18.18% out of 55) Homini of Indeterminate Biological Sex Recovered as Single (7 or 70.0 % out of 10), and Multiple (3 or 30.0% out of 10) Interments

GRAPH 9

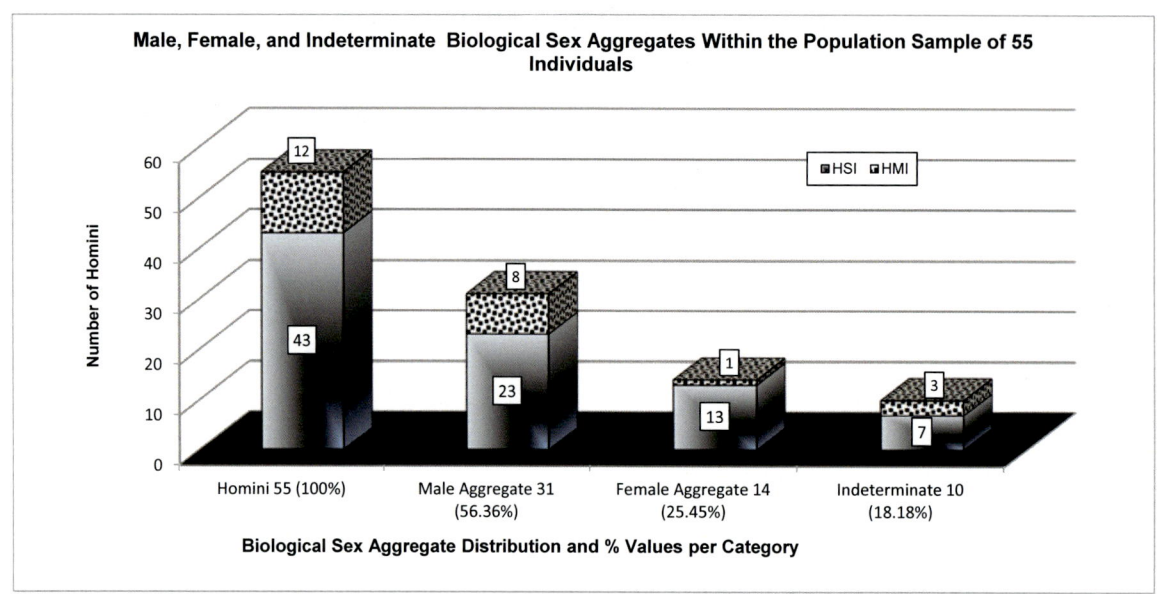

GRAPH 10

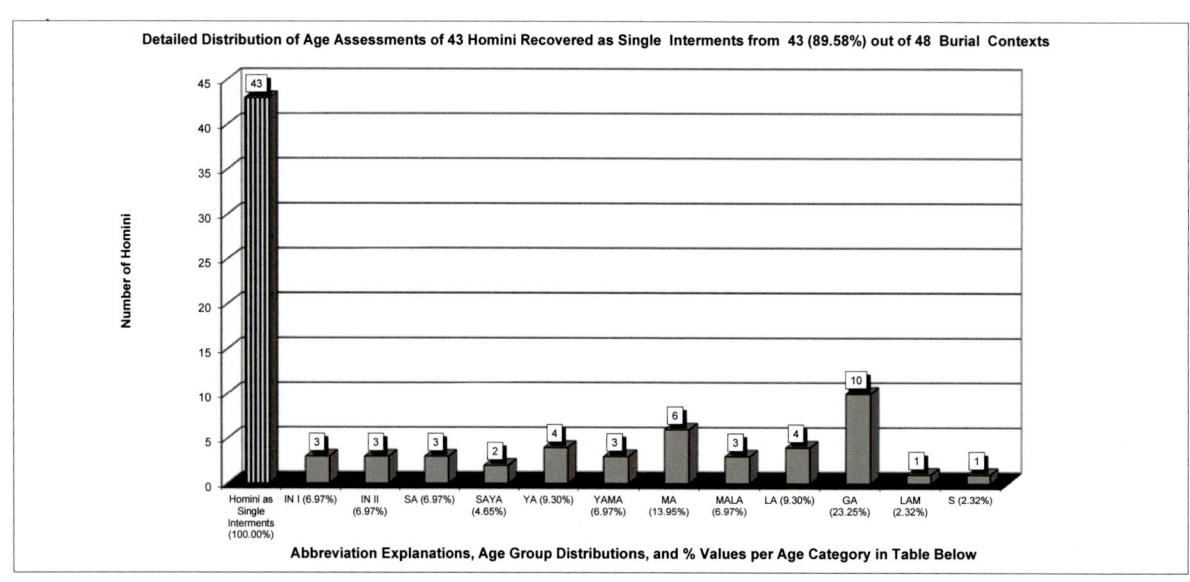

GRAPH 11

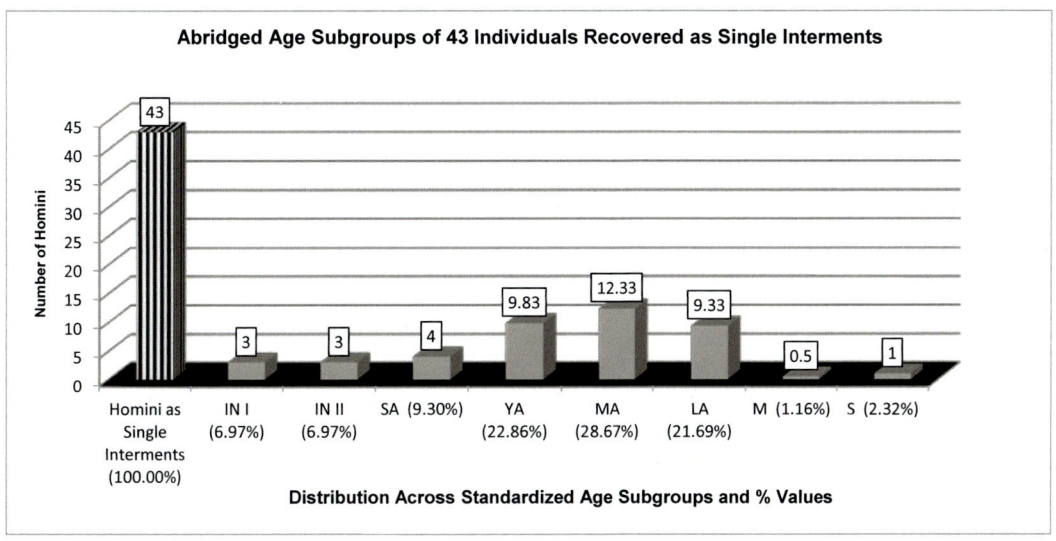

GRAPH 12

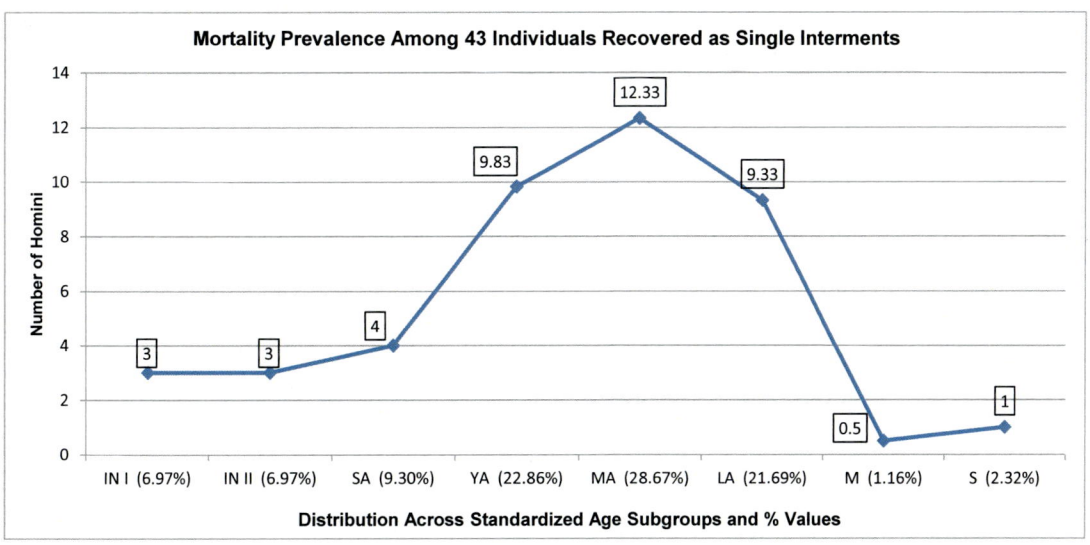

GRAPH 13

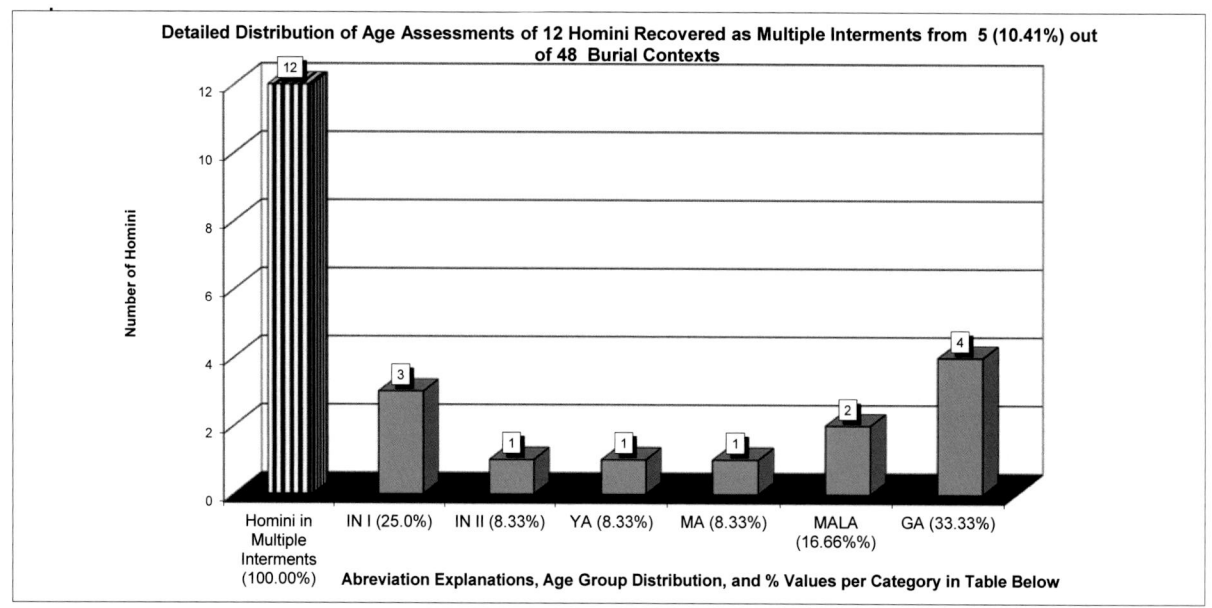

GRAPH 14

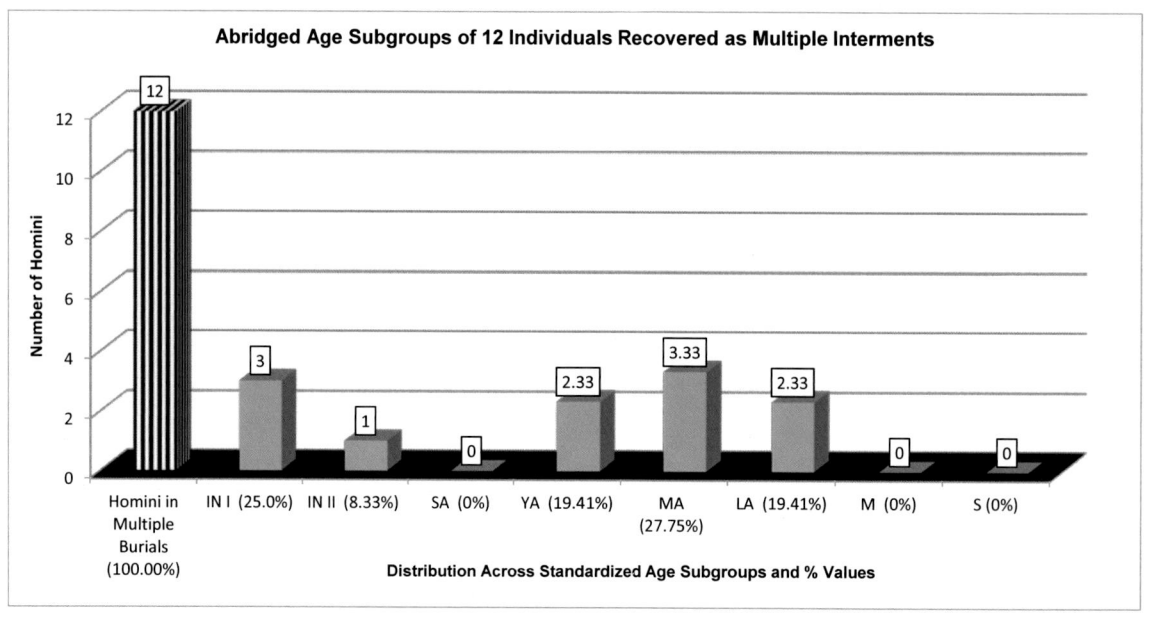

GRAPH 15

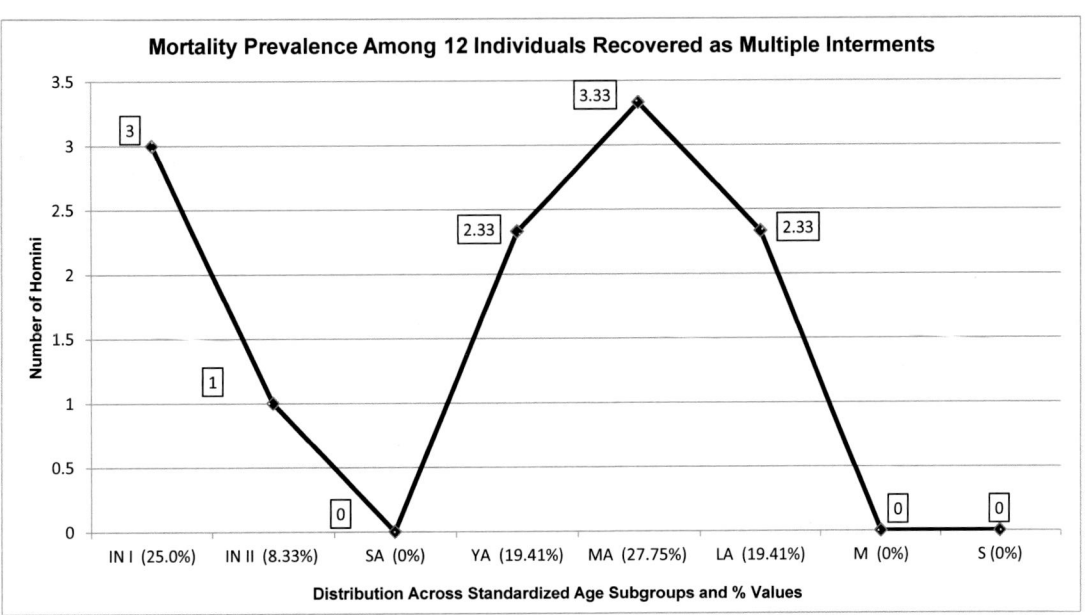

GRAPH 16

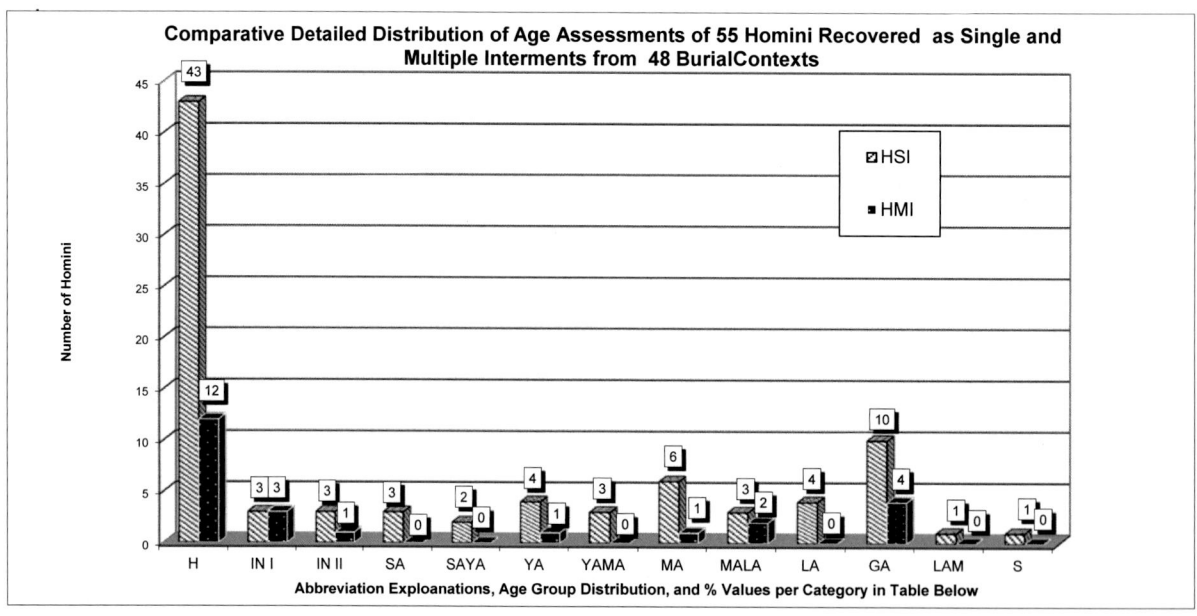

GRAPH 17

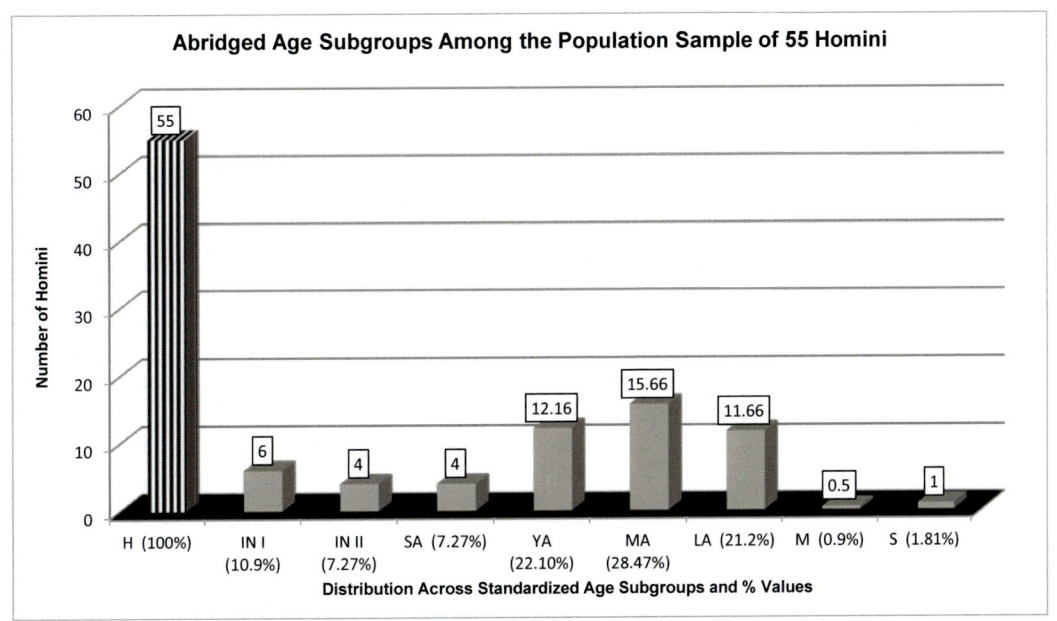

GRAPH 18

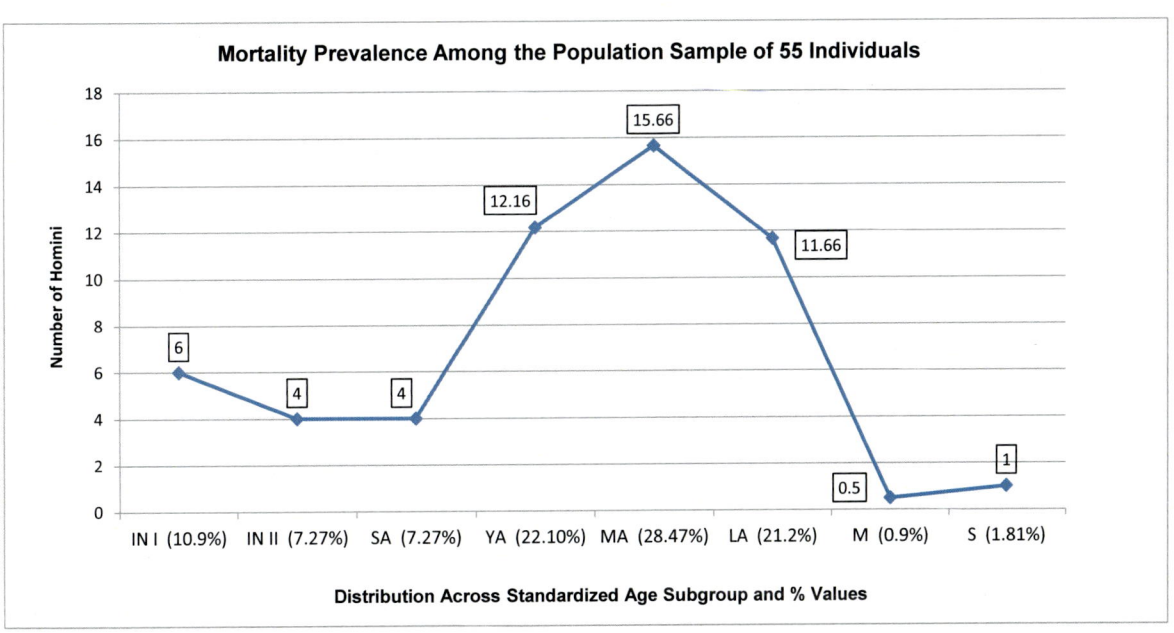

GRAPH 19

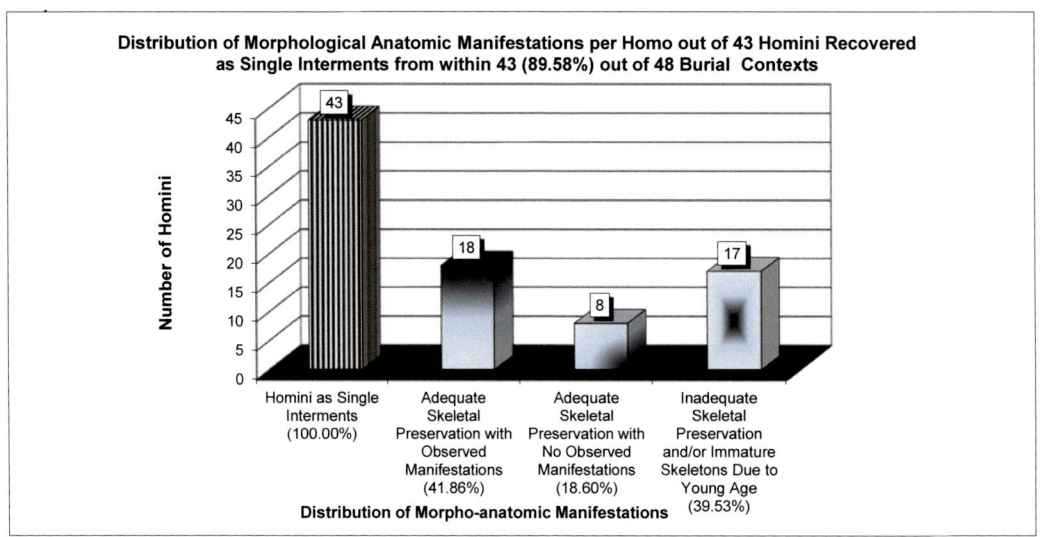

GRAPH 20

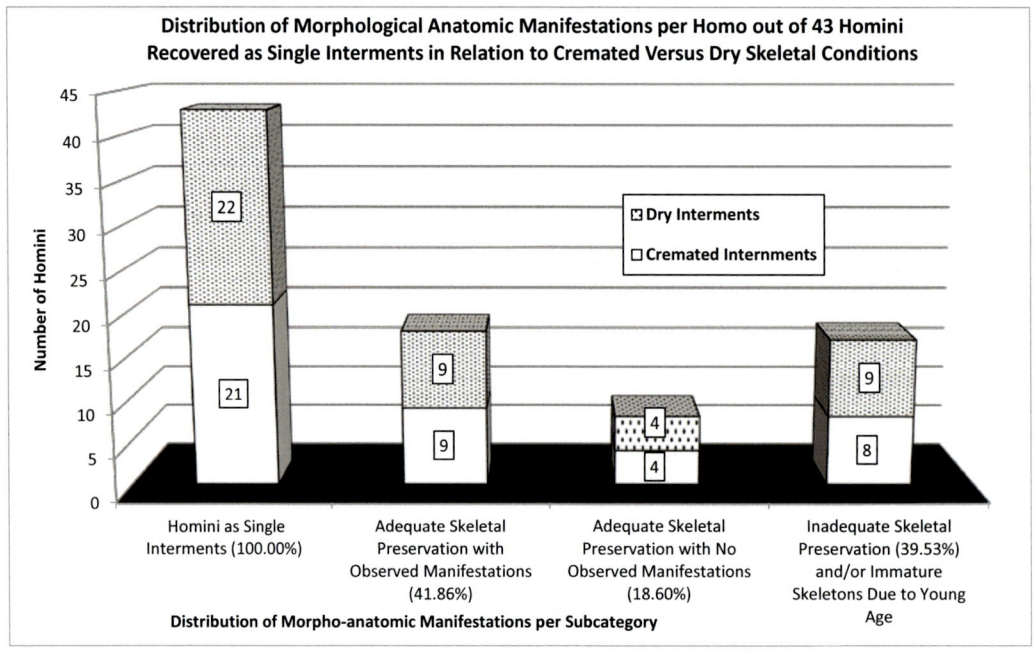

GRAPH 20A

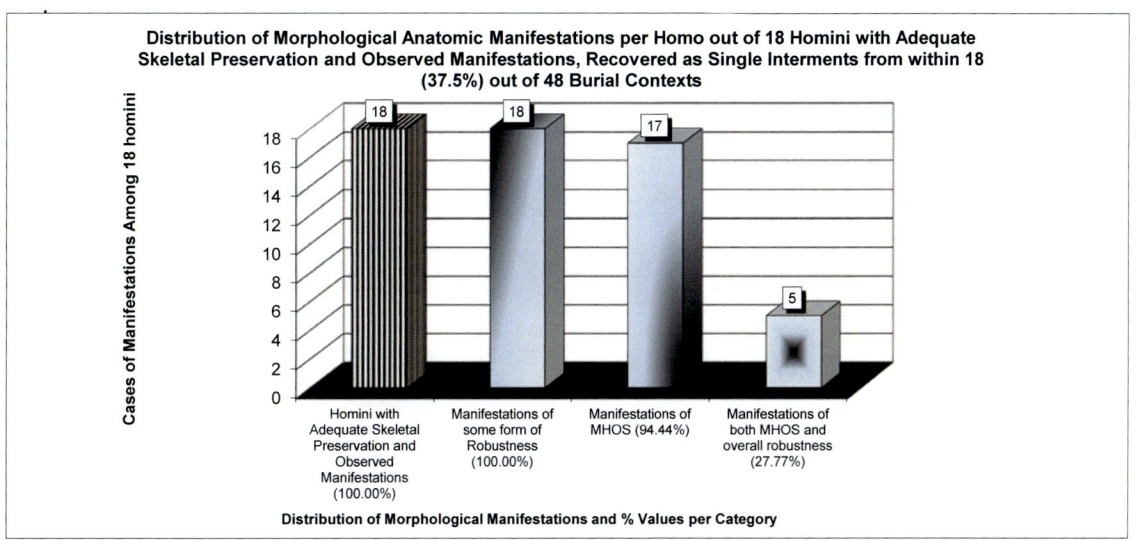

GRAPH 21

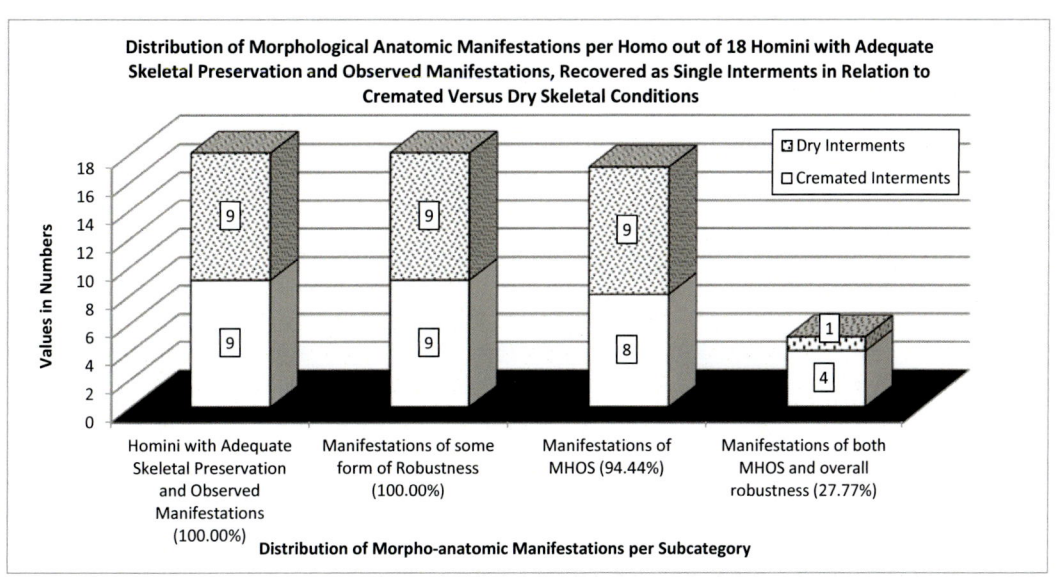

GRAPH 21A

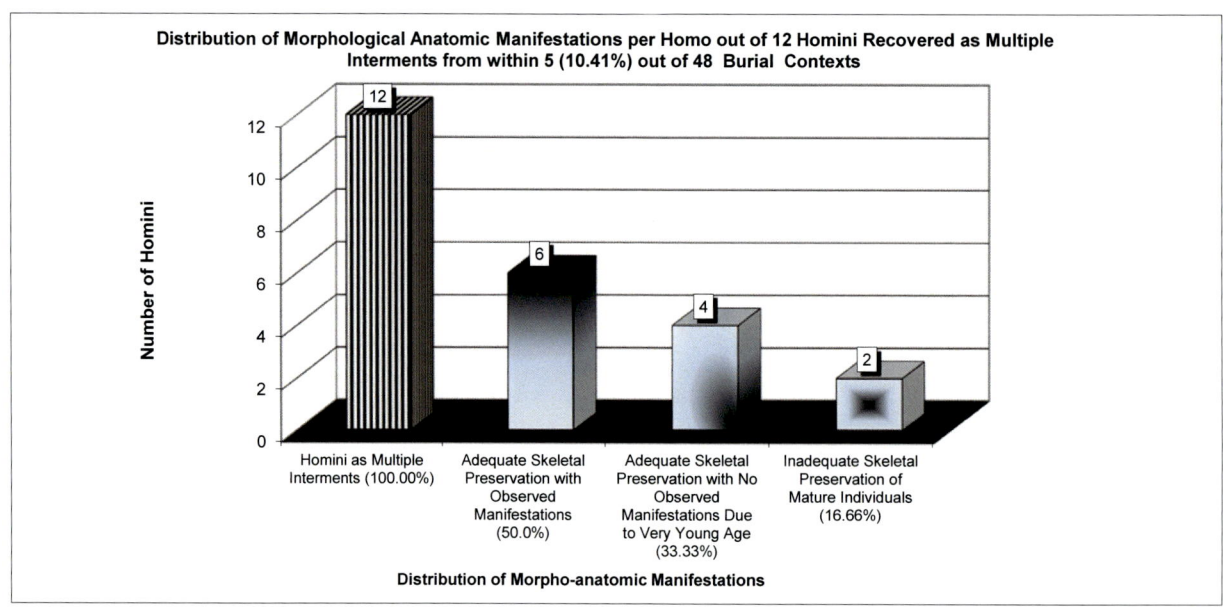

GRAPH 22

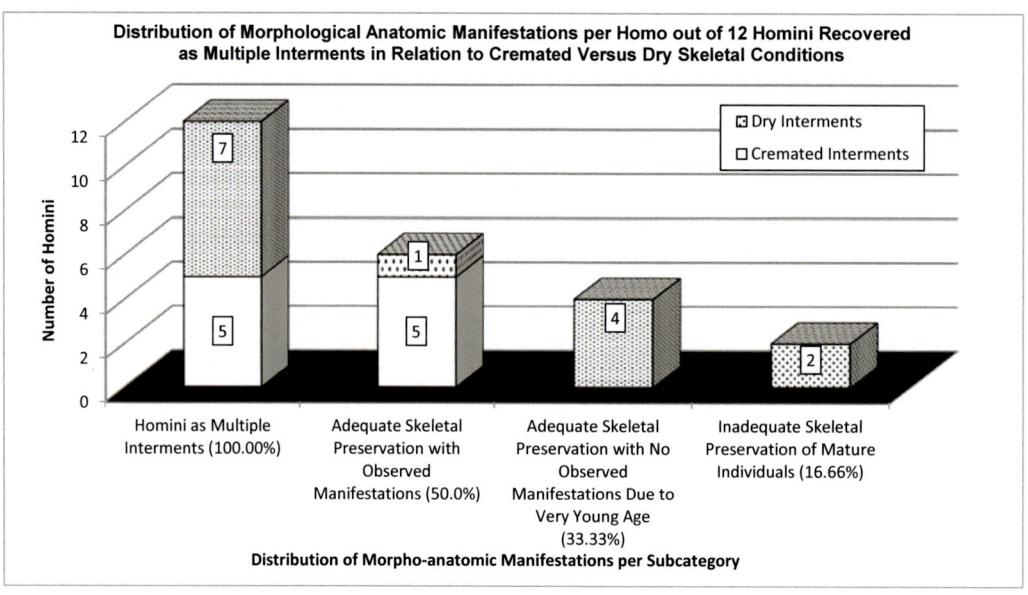

GRAPH 22A

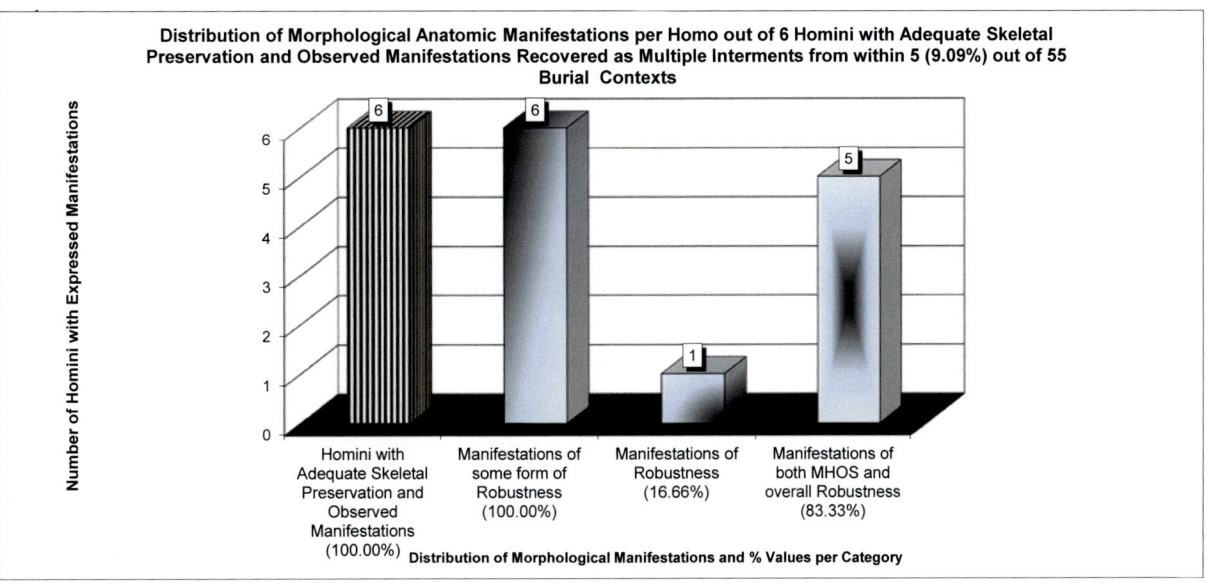

GRAPH 23

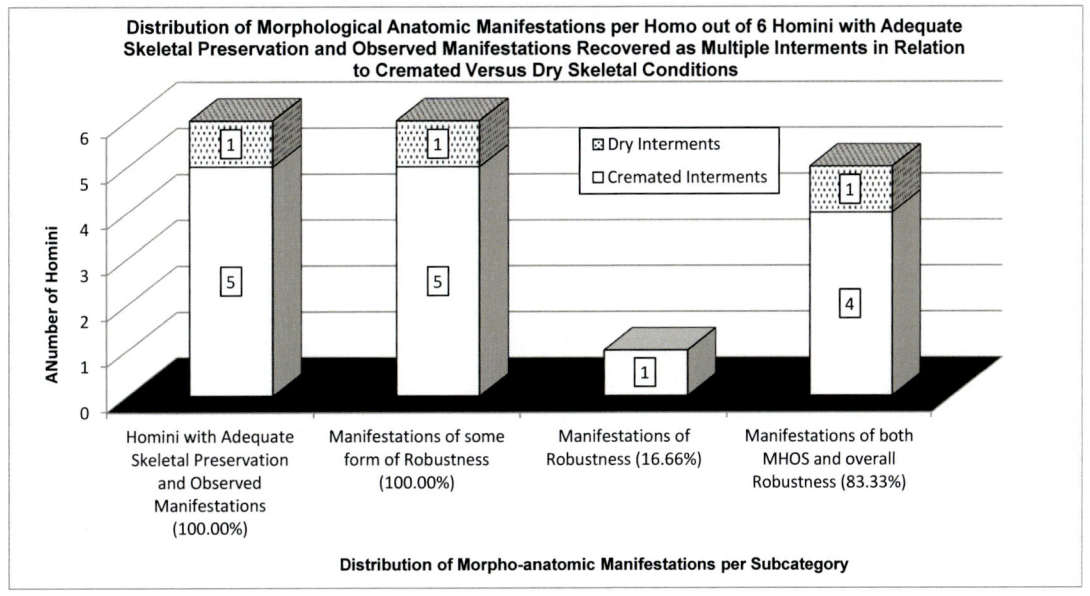

GRAPH 23A

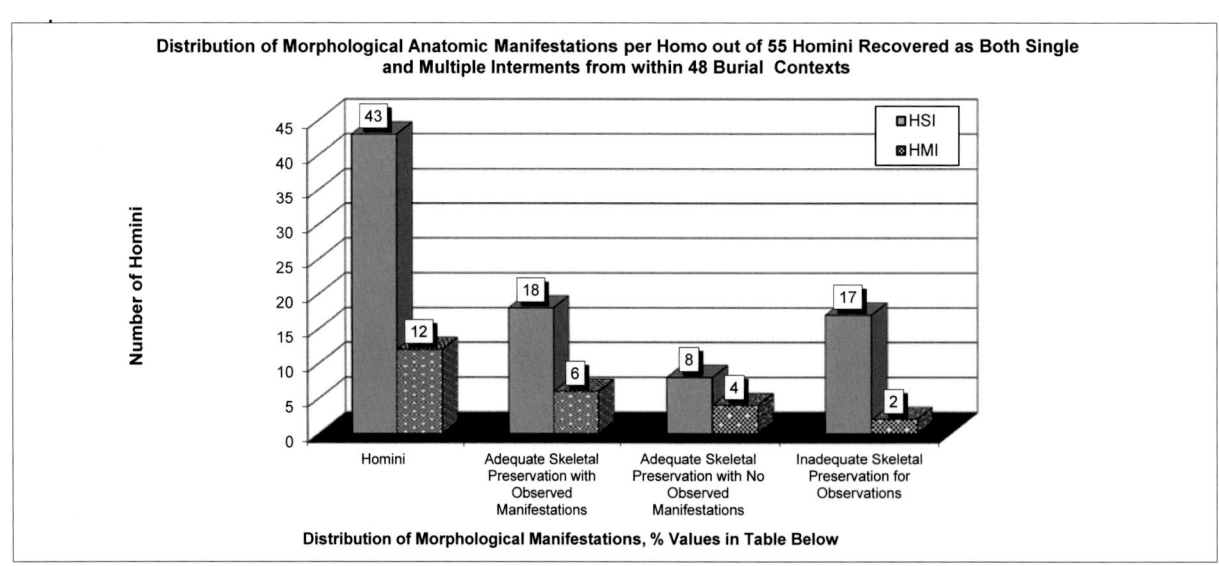

GRAPH 24

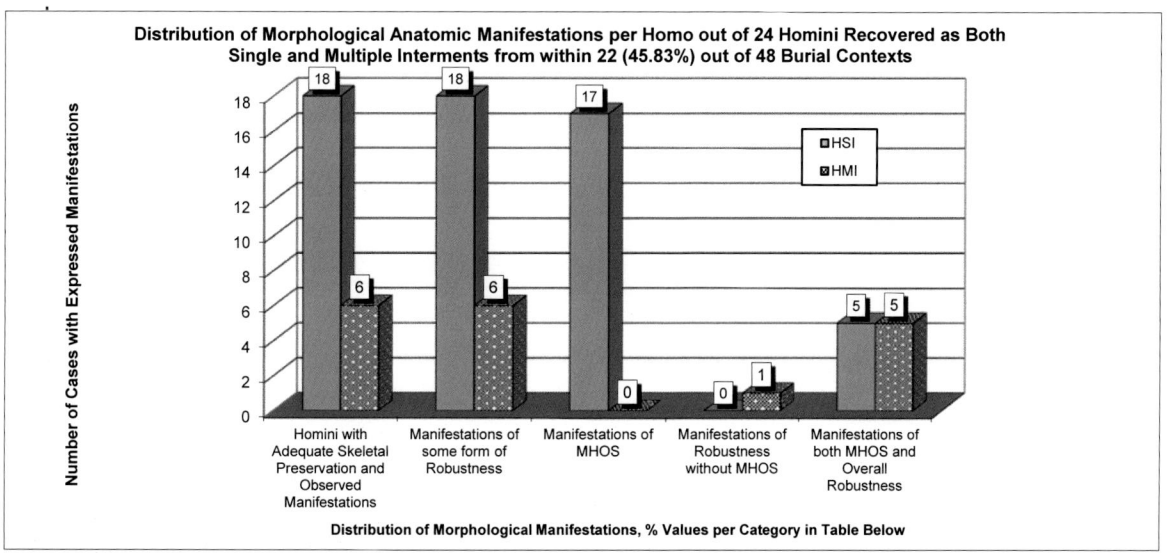

Values per Subcategory		
Homini with Adequate Skeletal Preservation and Observed Manifestations	=	Remains of 24 Homini with Adequate Skeletal Preservation and Observed Manifestations as Single (18 or 75.0% out of 24), and Multiple (6 or 25.0% out of 24) Interments
Manifestations of some form of Robustness	=	Remains of 24 Homini with Adequate Skeletal Preservation and Observed Manifestations as Single (18 or 75.0% out of 24), and Multiple (6 or 25.0% out of 24) Interments
Manifestations of MHOS	=	Remains of 17 Homini with Manifestations of MHOS as Single (17 or 94.44% out of 18 homini which showed manifestations of some form of robustness) Interments
Manifestations of Robustness without MHOS	=	Remains of 1 Homo with Manifestations of Robustness without MHOS from the Multiple (1 or 16.66% out of 6 homini which showed some form of robustness) Interments
Manifestations of both Robustness and MHOS	=	Remains of 10 Homini with Manifestations of both Robustness and MHOS as Single (5 or 50.0% out of 10), and Multiple (5 or 50.0% out of 10) Interments

GRAPH 25

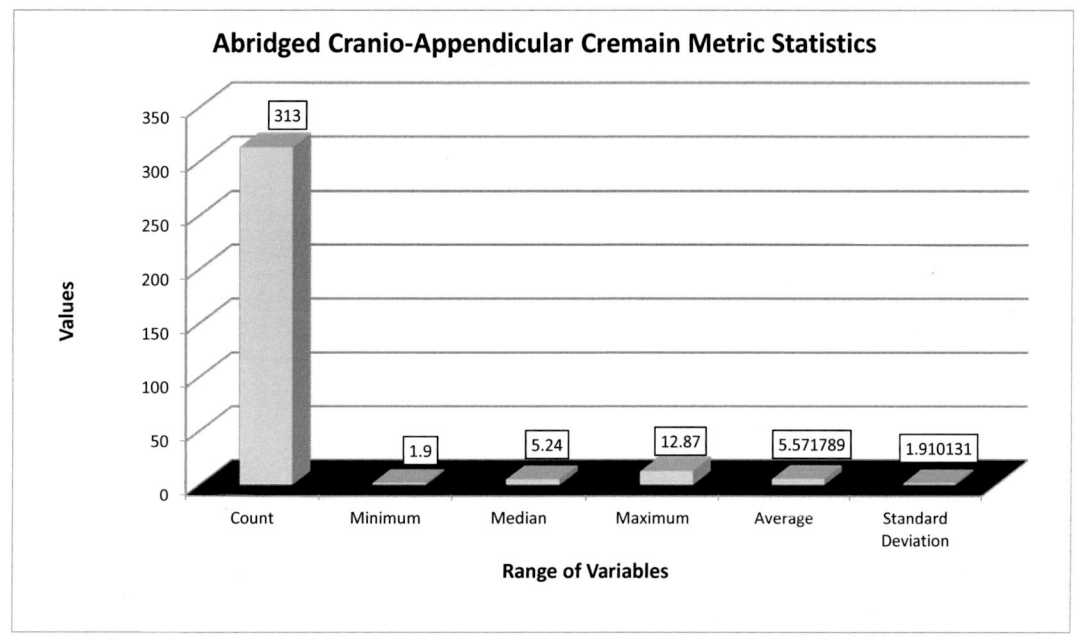

GRAPH 26

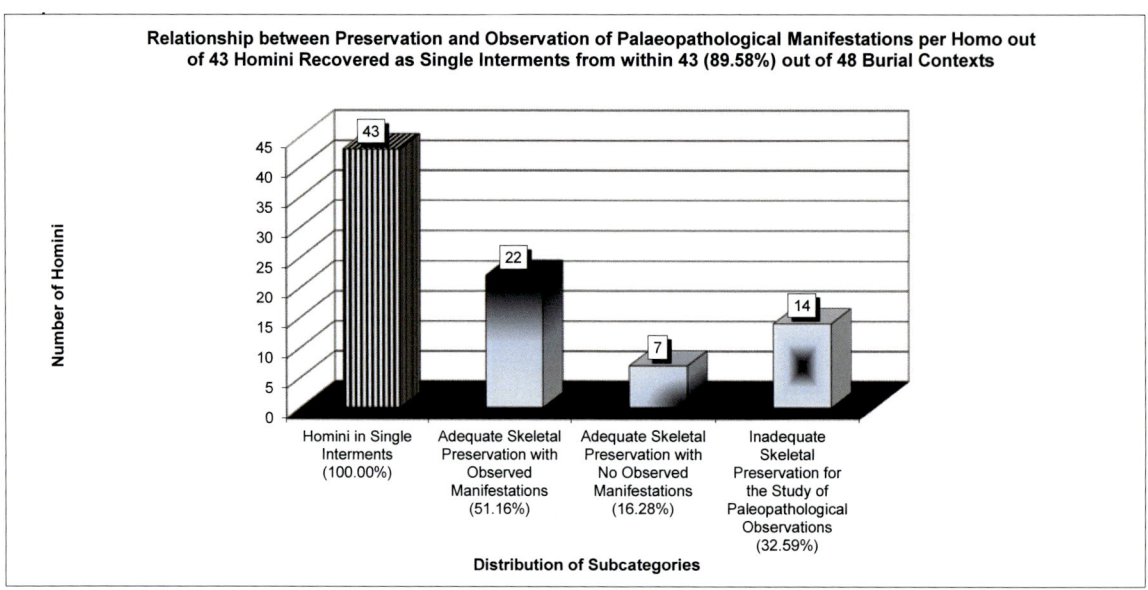

GRAPH 27

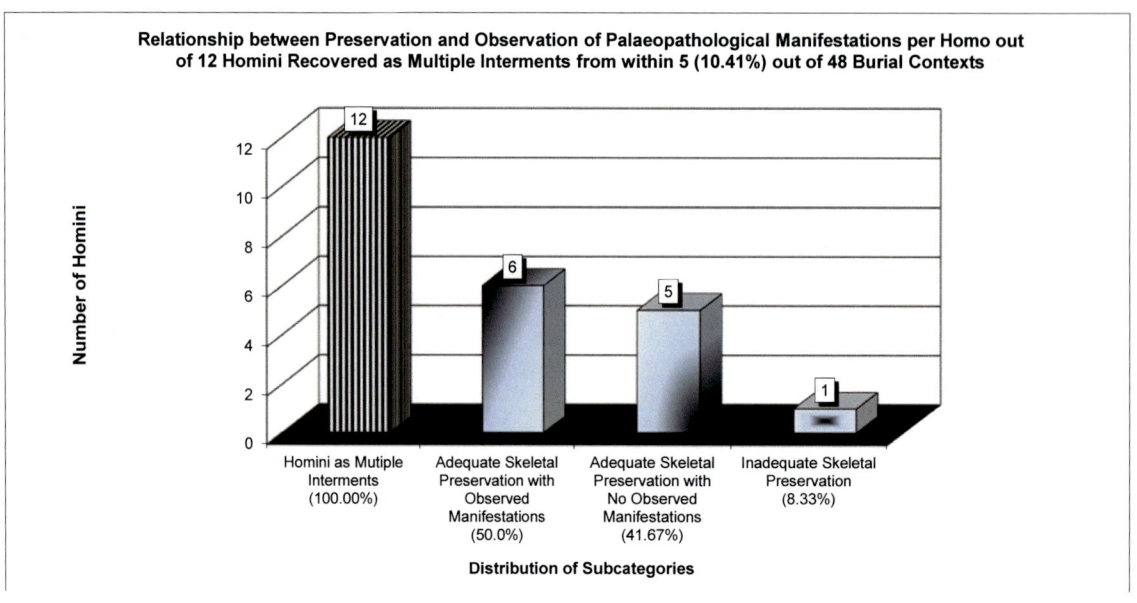

GRAPH 28

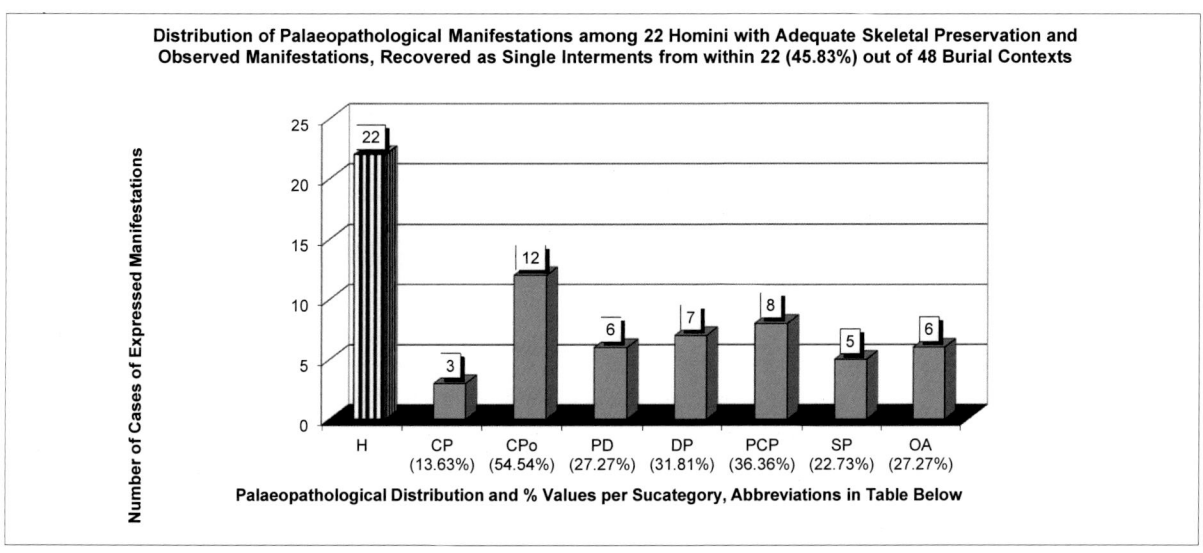

GRAPH 29

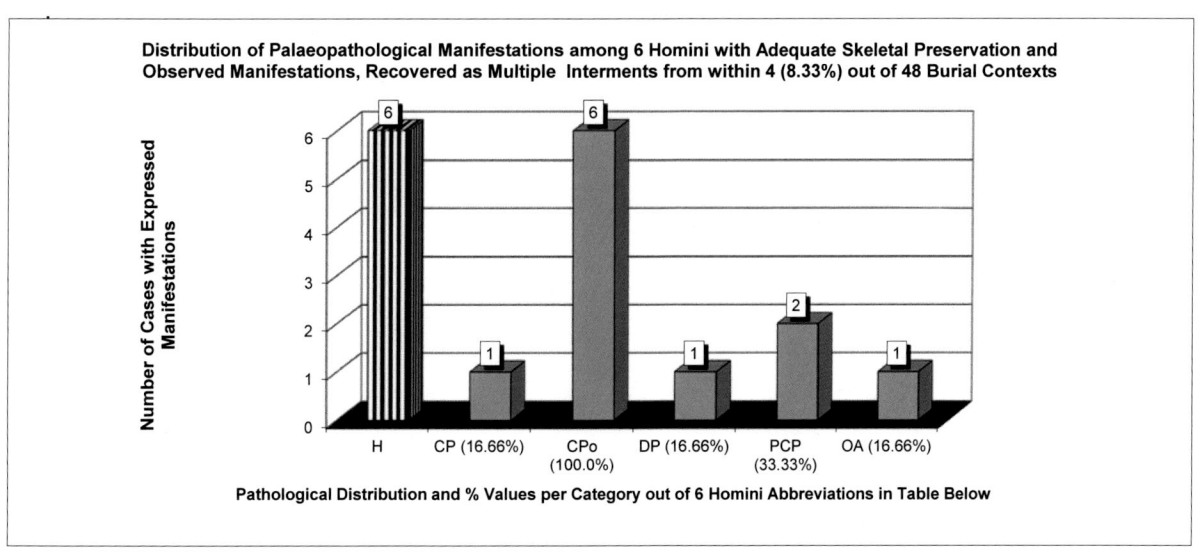

GRAPH 30

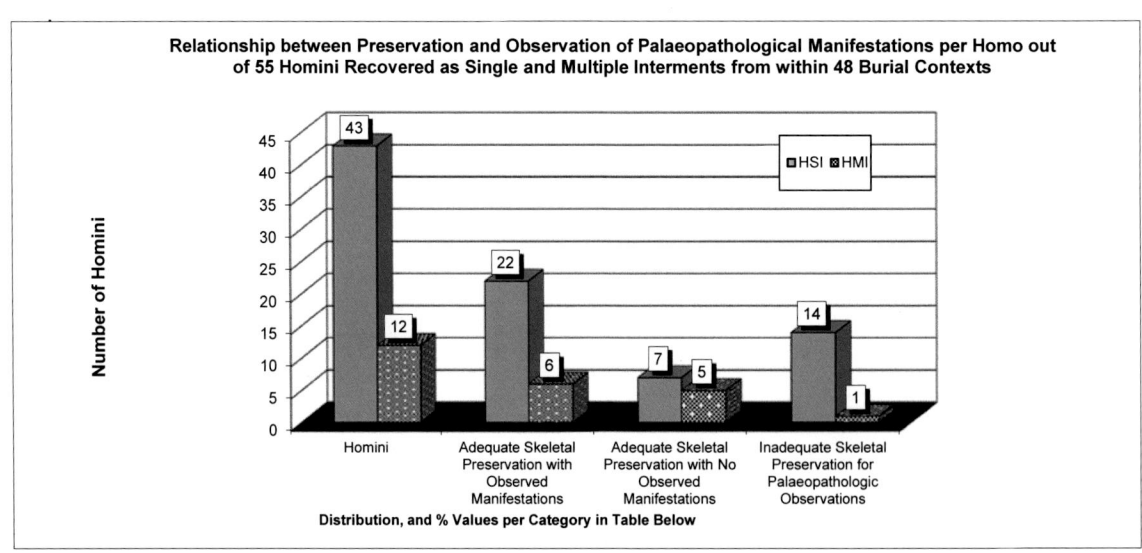

Distribution and % Values per Subcategory		
Homini	=	Remains of 55 Homini as Single (43) and Multiple (12) Interments
Adequate Skeletal Preservation with Observed Manfestations	=	28 (50.9% out of 55) Homini with Adequate Skeletal Preservation and Observed Manifestations as Single (22 or78.57 % out of 28), and Multiple (6 or 21.42% out of 28) Interments
Adequate Skeletal Preservation with No Observed Manifestations	=	12 (21.81% out of 55) Homini with Adequate Skeletal Preservation and No Observed Manifestations as Single (7 or 58.33% out of 12), and Multiple (5 or 41.66% out of 12) Interments
Inadequate Skeletal Preservation for Palaeopathologic Study	=	15 (27.27% out of 55) Homini with Inadequate Skeletal Preservation as Single (14 or 93.33% out of 15), and Multiple (1 or 6.66% out of 15) Interments

GRAPH 31

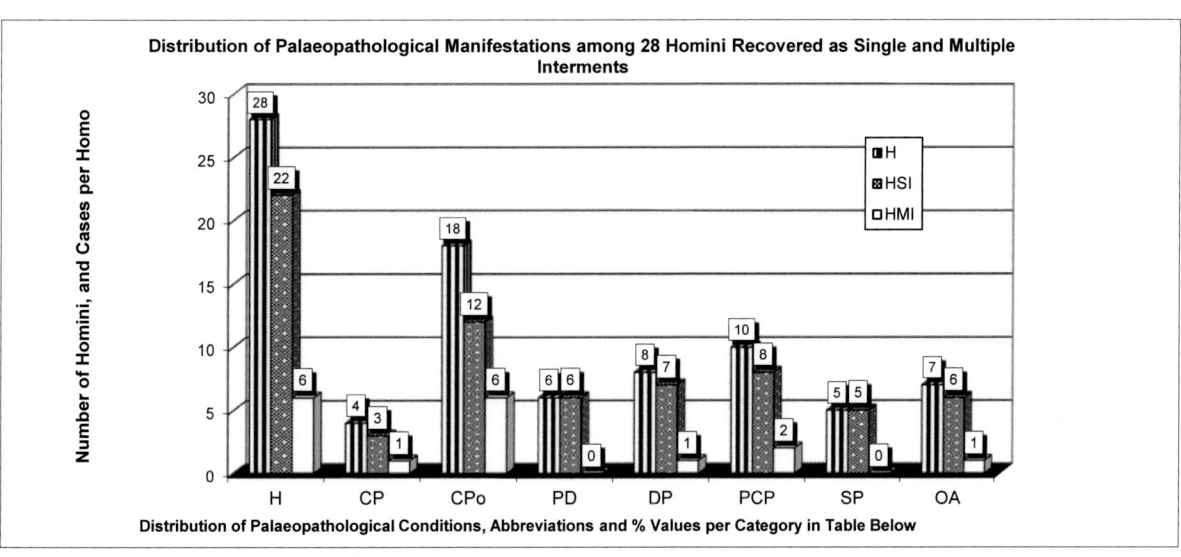

GRAPH 32

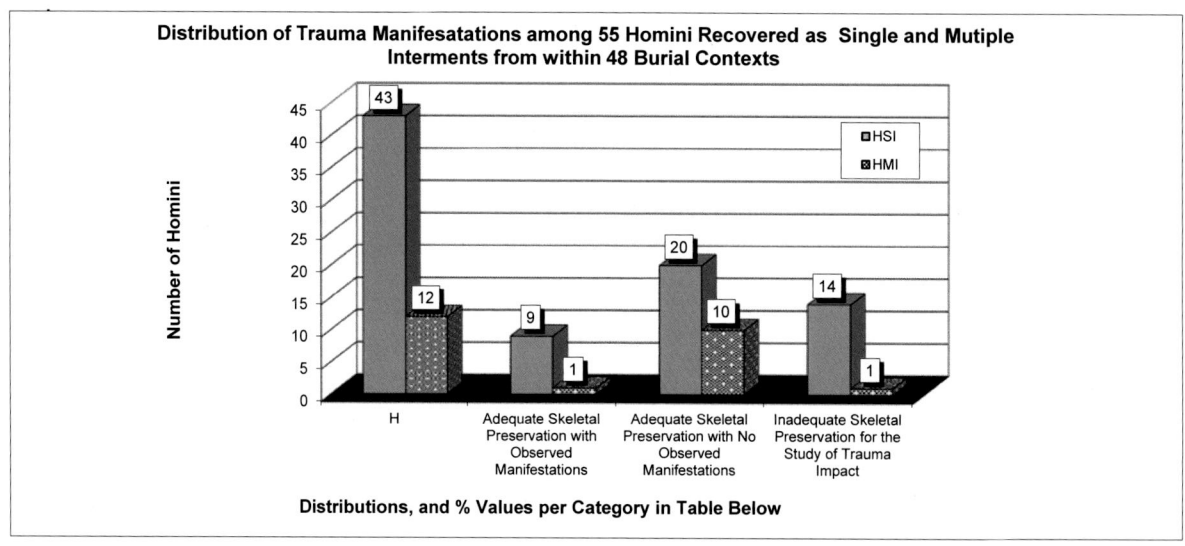

GRAPH 33

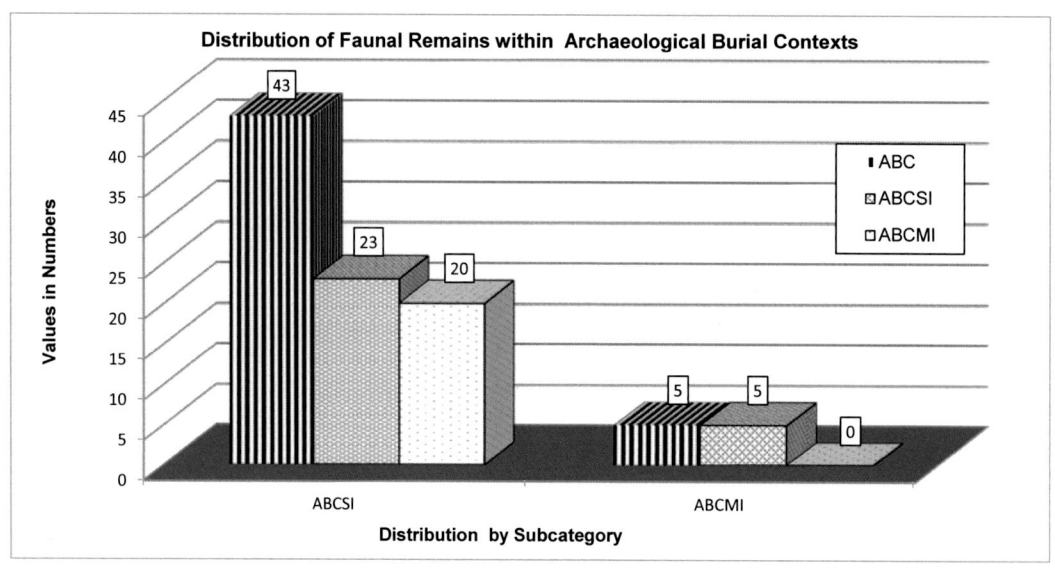

GRAPH 34

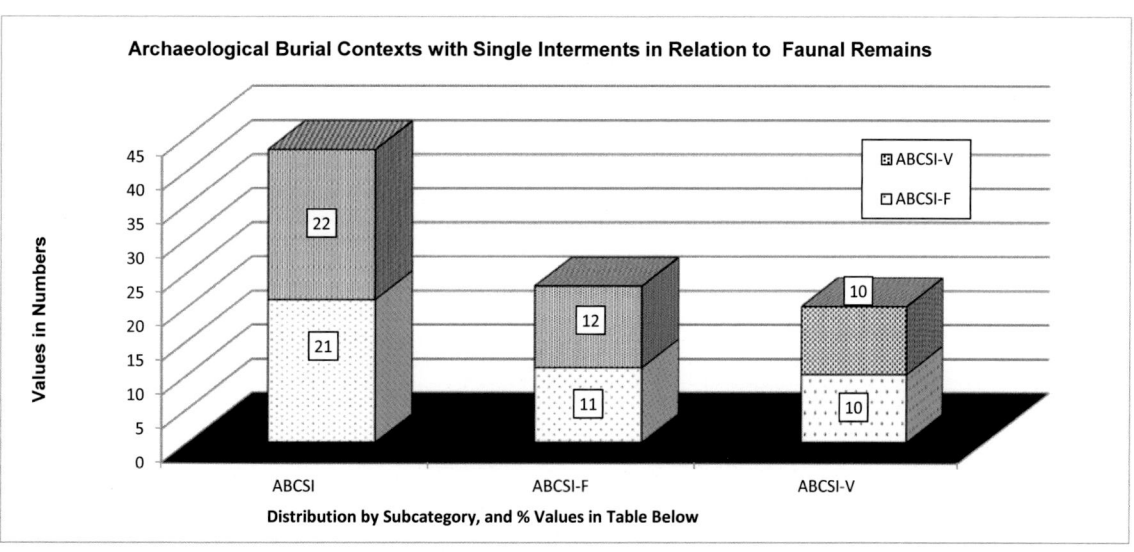

ABCSI = Archaeological Burial Contexts with Single Interments	=	43 Contexts which Yielded 21 (48.84%) Homini in Cremated Form, and 22 (51.16%) Homini in Dry Form
ABCSI-F = Archaeological Burial Contexts with Single Interments Associated with Faunal Remains	=	11 Contexts with Single Cremated Interments (52.38% out of 21, and 25.58% out of the 43) Associated with Faunal Remains, and 12 Contexts with Single Dry Interments (54.54% out of 22, and 27.90% out of 43) Associated with Faunal Remains
ABCSI-V = Archaeological Burial Contexts with Single Interments Void of Faunal Remains	=	10 Contexts with Single Cremated Interments (47.62% out of 21 and 23.25% out of the 43) Void of Faunal Remains, and 10 Contexts with Single Dry Interments (45.45% out of 22, and 23.25% out of 43) Void of Faunal Remains

GRAPH 35

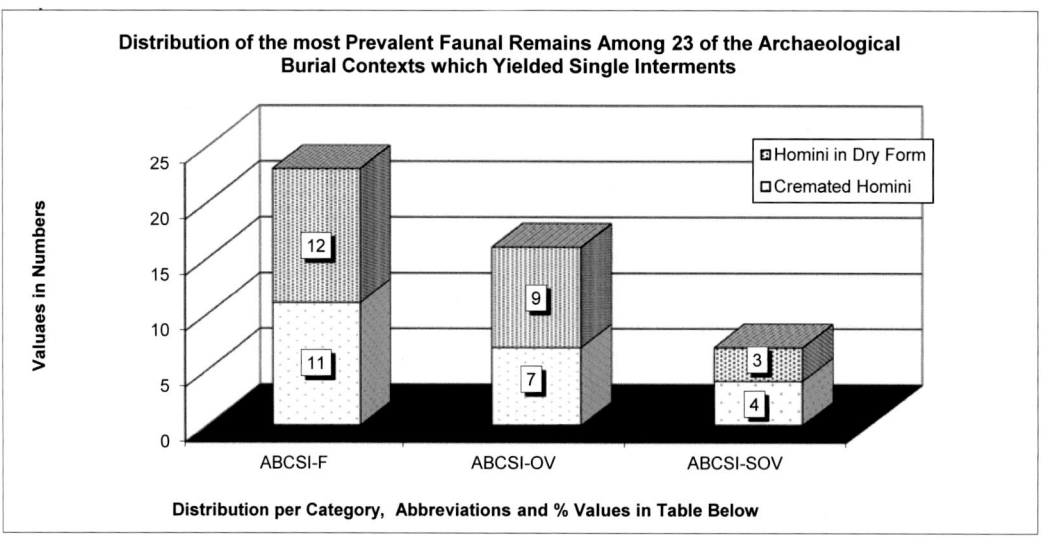

ABCSI-F = Archaeological Burial Contexts with Single Interments Associated with Faunal Remains	=	23 Contexts with Single Interments Comprising 11 (47.83% out of 23) Homini in Cremated Form and 12 (52.17% out of 23) in Dry Form Associated with Faunal Remains
ABCSI-OV = Archaeological Burial Contexts with Single Interments Associated with Ovicaprical Remains	=	16 Contexts with Single Interments Comprising 7 (43.75% out of 16) Homini in Cremated Form and 9 (56.25% out of 16) in Dry Form Associated with Ovicaprical Offerings
ABCSI-SOV = Archaeological Burial Contexts with Single Interments Associated with Suspected Ovicaprical Remains	=	7 Contexts with Single Interments Comprising 4 (57.14% out of 7) Homini in Cremated Form and 3 (42.86% out of 7) in Dry Form Associated with Suspected Ovicaprical Offerings

GRAPH 36

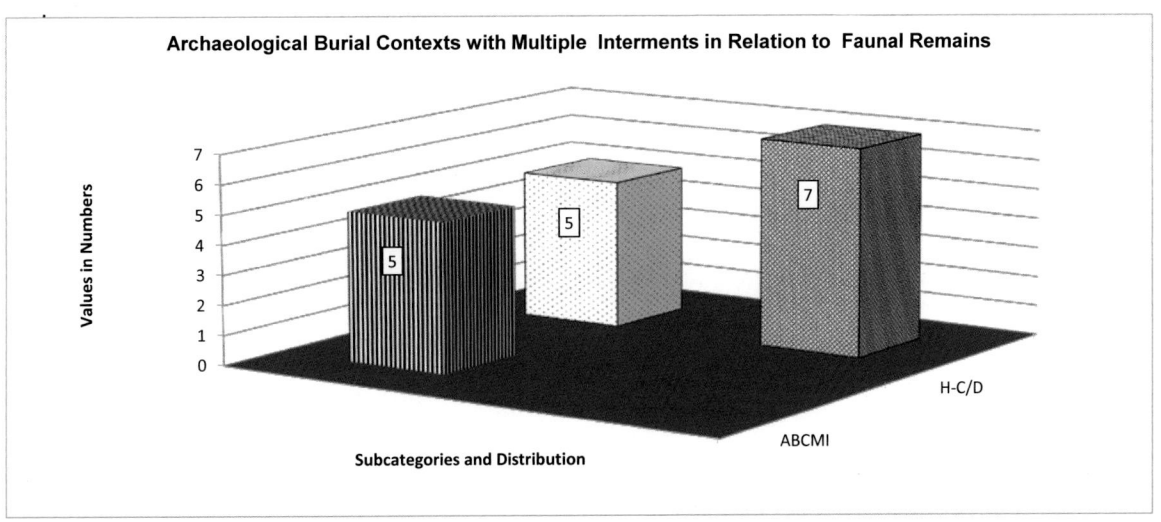

Graph Abbreviation Explanations, and % Values per Category		
ABCMI = Archaeological Burial Contexts with Multiple Interments	=	5 Contexts which Yielded 12 Homini in Cremated and Dry Form, Associated with Faunal Remains
H-C = Cremated Homini	=	5 Cremated Homini with Associated Faunal Remains
H-D = Homini in Dry Form	=	7 Homini in Dry Form Associated with Faunal Remains

GRAPH 37

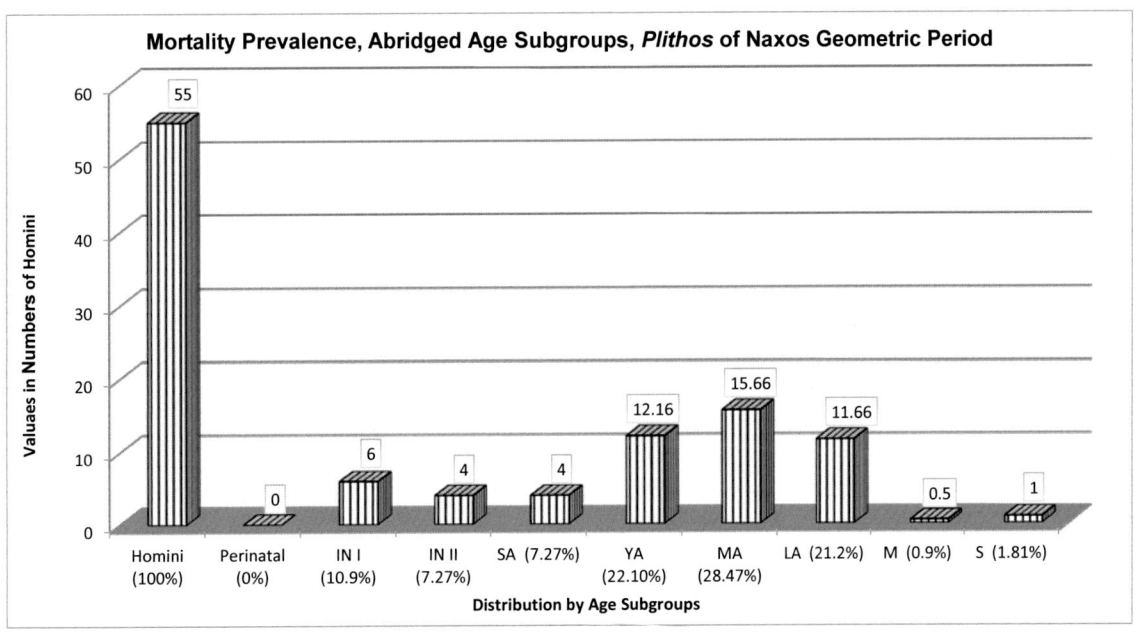

GRAPH 38

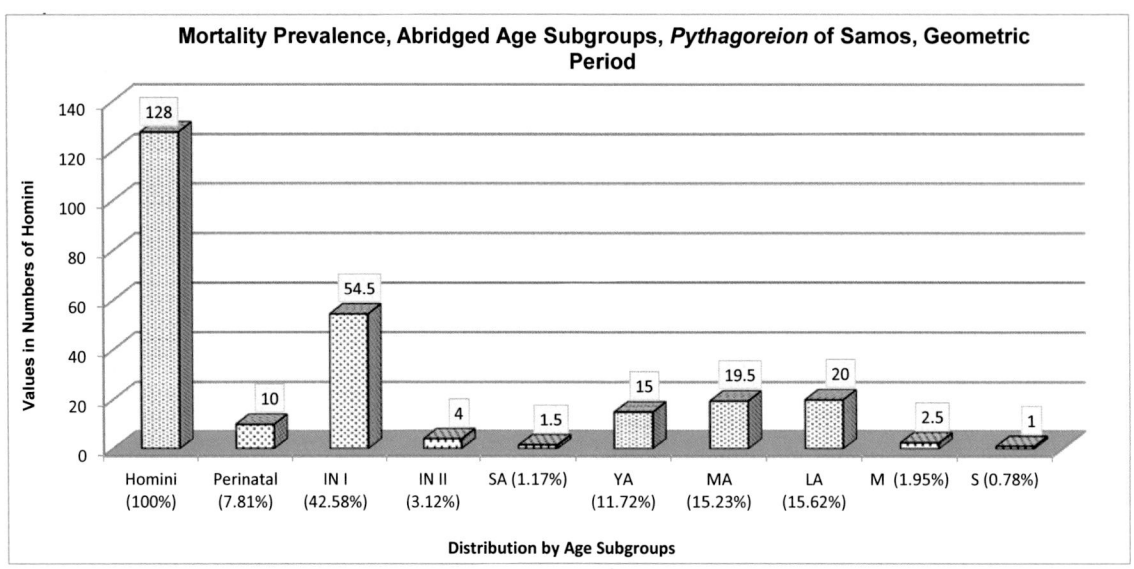

GRAPH 39

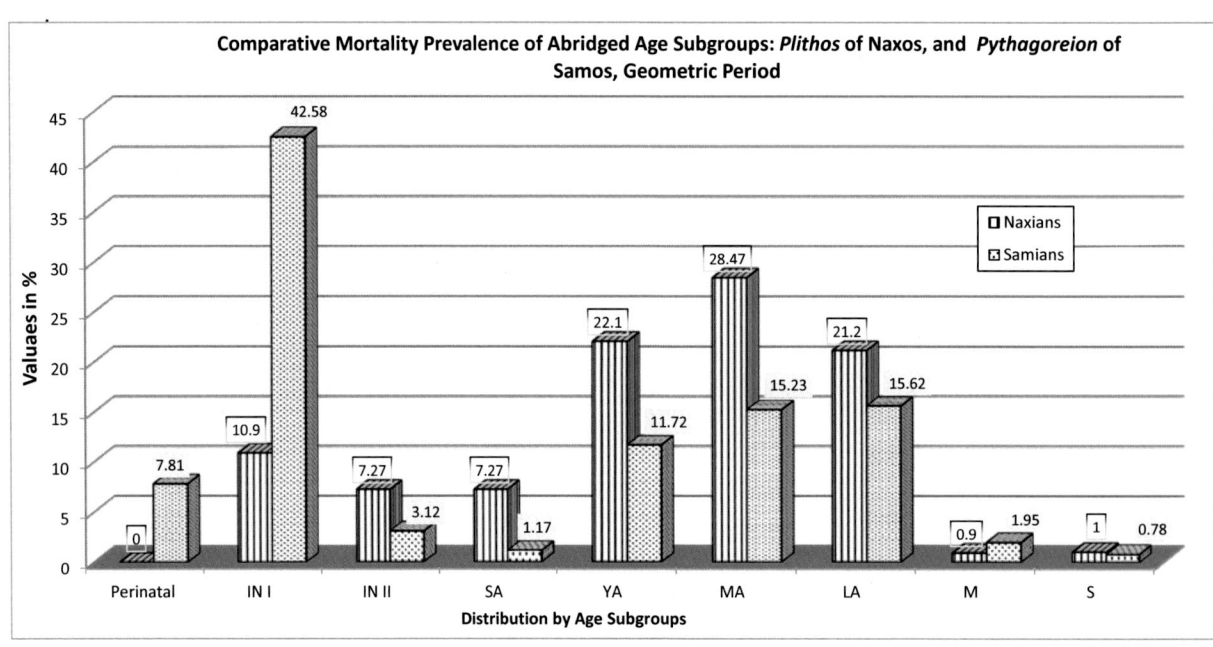

GRAPH 40

Tables

TABLE 1

Lab No.	Burial No. in Arabic	Burial No in Latin Numerals or other Contextual Data	Assessment of Labs with same contextual data	Intrusive Homo	Intended Burial-Homo	C/D	Remains	Cremation Level	Faunal	Ecofactual	Artifactual	Biological Sex	Age	Morphology	Pathology	Trauma	Weight (gr)
1	44	Oikopedo Axiopoulou, Square 2, 14/8/78				Dry	CDPA	--	none	none	none	Female	YA	MHOS	DP, CPo, CP	CT	
2		Oikopedo Axiopoulou, pliThos, 6 grave VI, xsa, 3/10/77				Dry	CDPA	--	dry ovicaprical mandible fragment	none	none	Female	MA	MHOS	PD	None observed	
3		Oikopedo Axiopoulou, Square 6, 51 burial LI, Jar ΓΙ4				Dry	CDPAA	--	two tibial fragments of large dry ovicaprical	none	none	Possible Female	TIN II	None due to limited preservation		None observed	
4		LVIII, X6, Oik. Axaopouleu, Bones, 28/8/78 (Lab 4); "D" grave LVIII, Bones of deceased 58 (Lab 30)	Labs # 4 and 30 are of the same context		Homo 1	Dry	CPAA	--	dry ovicaprical lower jaw and vertebral plates and long bones of younger faunal	none	none	Male	MALA	Robust, MHOS	OA, CPo, PCP	SN, PCT	730.00
30	58		Labs # 4 and 30 are of the same context		Homo 2	Dry	CDPAA	--	dry ovicaprical tooth incisor	none	none	Possible Male	IN II	None observed	DP, CPo	None observed	
5		Oikopedo, S. Kambysi, NΛ Ta 44 28, Grave LII				Cremated	CDPAA	Well cremated to a sub-calcined degree	none	none	fragment and iron fragments adhered to conglomerates	Male	MALA	Robust, MHOS	PCP	None observed	64.00
6		Oikopedo Kambysi, 8/8/78 Tafros E, Grave XXXIX, bones of 39 the skeleton				Dry	CDPAA	--	none	none	none	Female	S	Robust, MHOS	PD, DP, SP, OA, PCP	None observed	
7	53	Oikopedo Kambysi, burial IIII				Cremated	CPApp	Cremated to a sub-calcined degree	none	none	none	Male	GA	Robust, MHOS	None observed	None observed	64.00
8	49	Oikopedo B. Axiopoulou Δ. Burial XLIX				Cremated	CPApp	Cremated to a sub-calcined degree	none	none	none	Male	GA	None due to limited preservation	None due to limited preservation	None due to limited preservation	187.00
9	29	Oikopedo Axiopoulou, Δ burial XXIX, bones of the fire laye				Cremated	CD	Cremated to a sub-calcined degree	none	none	none	Probable Male	YA	None due to limited preservation	None due to limited preservation	None due to limited preservation	13.00
10		Oikopedo Axaopoulou, Square Δ, South Corner, Amphora Π1_ Bones from the inside				Cremated	CDPApp	Cremated to a sub-calcined degree	none	none	none	Male	MALA	None due to limited preservation	None due to limited preservation	None due to limited preservation	188.00
11	19	Oikopedo Axiopoulou, Ta XIK, bones within amphora				Cremated	CDPAA	Well cremated to a sub-calcined degree	none	none	Pottery fragment	Male	LA	MHOS	OA	None observed	822.00
12	34	XXXIV, Oik. Axaopoulou, Square G', Grave XXXIV, bones around pyre and values (Lab 12); Bones & Charcoal (lab 50)	Labs # 12 and 50 are the same context and Homo.			Cremated	CPAA	Cremated to a sub-calcined degree	cremated faunal remains (animal bone with buthering/cut marks	Rocks	Ceramic fragments, one showing a decorative motif	Male	MA	None observed	None observed	None observed	216.00
13	37	Oikopedo Axiopoulou, Square G, XXXVII, Amphora Π1. Bones within amphora.				Cremated	CDPAA	Cremated to a sub-calcined/calcined degree	none	Shells	none	Male	LA	None observed	PD, PCP	None observed	428.00
14		Oikopedo B' Axiopoulou, 28/8/78, Building θ, bones				Dry	C (parietal fragment with open sutures)		mandibular, cranial, and endocranial fragments of most likely of a dry ovicaprical	none	none	Probable Male	YAMA	None observed	None observed	None observed	
15	28	Oikopedo Axiopoulou, burial ground, 4/8/78 Square A, grave XXVIII, bones of Π1				Dry	CPAA	--	none	none	none	Indeterminate	IN I	None due to limited preservation	CPo	None observed	
16	13b	Oikopedo Axiopoulou, Γ', "af." XIIIβ, bones, depth- C.33				Cremated	CDPAA	Cremated to a sub-calcined degree	none	none	A large core of iron, most probably from a nail	Male	MA	None observed	SP	PCT, SN	149.00
17		Oikopedo B. Axiopoulou 16/8/'78 Δ. Grave XXIII, fragment of the 23 lower jaw				Dry	Only the R. side of mandible w/ dentitions in situ)		none	none	none	Indeterminate (Possible Male)	IN II	None observed	DP	None observed	

#	Context	Notes	Sub-id	Condition	Code	Cremation degree	Faunal remains	Other	Grave goods	Sex	Age	Robusticity	Pathology	Other path.	Weight
18	Oikopedo S. Kambysi, 22/8/78, βA, layering around Cut A east section, depth ±0.00 bones			Dry	CDPApp	—	none	none	none	Possible Male	SA	None observed	CPo	None observed	
19	Oikopedo Axiopoulou, Square Γ, Taf. XXXVI, from amphora Π1			Cremated	CDPAA	Cremated to a sub-calcined degree	none	none	none	Male	YA	MHOS	PD, CPo	PCT	479.00
20	XXXVIII, Oikopedo Kambysi, Tafros E, 7/8/78	Included an additional Homo DRY, a tibial distal frag and a metatarsal, Adult, indeterminate sex		Dry	CPAA	—	none	none	Two pottery fragments	Indeterminate	IN I	None observed	CPo, PCP	None observed	
21	Border Cut β and βA projection Tafrou A, Taf. LVII, South T31, 57 Depth -.50			Cremated	PApp	Cremated to a sub-calcined degree	dry faunal remains (large horn-core fragment most likely of a male ovicaprical individual	none	none	Male	GA	None due to limited preservation	None due to limited preservation	None due to limited preservation	94.00
22	Oikopedo Axiopoulou, Square 2, Bones, +0.55	Included an additional Homo DRY, few tibial frags, <16 years, indeterminate sex		Cremated	C	Cremation was non homogeneous: thermally altered to a calcined degree	dry ovicaprical bone fragments	none	none	Male	MALA	None due to limited preservation	None due to limited preservation	None due to limited preservation	47.00
23	Axiopoulou, Square E + 2, Taf. LXIV, Depth - 0.40-0.50			Cremated	CDPAA	Ranged from thermally altered to a calcined degree	none	Rock	none	Male	SA	None observed	None observed	None observed	301.00
24	XV, Oik. Axiopoulou, Square E, Grave XV, Bones of Jar Burial 15 "P"7, 30/8/78	Labs # 24, 28, and 35 are of the same context–Labs # 24 and 35 are the same Homo, Homo 1	Homo 1	Dry	CPAA	—	Dry Faunal frags	Marine shell and gastropod shell	none	Indeterminate	IN I	None due to limited preservation	CPo	None observed	
28	XV, Oik. Axiopoulou, Square E, Grave XV, Cranium of 15 Skeleton, 29/8/1978	Labs # 24, 28, and 35 are of the same context–Lab # 28 is Homo 2	Homo 2	Dry	C (parietal, temporal, occipital, and pars petrosae fragments)	—	none	none	none	Probable Male	MALA	None observed due to limited preservation	CPo, CP	None observed	
25	Oik. Axiopoulou, Square E + 2, 65 grave LXV, within Π1	Included an additional Homo, CREMATED, 1 frag at 1gr, Adult, indeterminate sex		Dry	CDPAA	—	dry long bone fragment of an ovicaprical	Shell fragment	none	Indeterminate	IN I	None observed	PCP	None observed	25.00
26	XLI, Oik. Kambysi, Tafros 2, 41 From within "P" 17, 12/8/78			Dry	CPAA	—	fragments of dry faunal, most likely ovicaprical	none	Cylindrical piece of iron	Indeterminate	IN I	None observed	CPo	None observed	45.00
26a	Cut 2, Grave XLI, from within "P" 17, 12/8/78			Cremated	PAA	—	none	none	none	Male	GA	Robust, MHOS	None observed	None observed	
27	Oik. Axiopoulou burial ground, 22 Square Γ, burial XXII, in 34			Cremated	CDPAA	Cremated to a sub-calcined degree	dry faunal remains (two fragments of an ovicaprical faunal)	none	none	Male	MA	MHOS	CPo, PCP	None observed	654.00

#	Context	Notes	Condition	Category	Degree of Cremation	Faunal Remains	Other Materials	Artifacts	Sex	Age	Fibula/Robustness	Pathology	Other Observations	Weight
29	Oik. Axiopoulou, Taf. XXXIII, 33 bones	Labs # 29 and 45 are the same context and Homo	Cremated	CPAA	Cremated from a sub-calcined degree to a calcined degree	thermally altered hare sized fragment, and dry ovicaprical faunal remains (large bovid dentition, rib, jaw fragment, horn-core fragment, and several other bovid astraglis long bone fragments	none	none	Male	GA	Robust Fibula	None due to limited preservation	None due to limited preservation	34.00
31	Oik. Axoupolou, Burial Ground, Square B, grave XXVII, 2/8/78, Charcoal. Depth -.055					none	Charcoal	none						25.00
32	XXIV, Oikopedo Axiopoluloum Grave XXIV, Bones		Homo 1	Cremated	CPAA	Cremated to a sub-calcined and almost calcined degree	dry ovicaprical remains (long tubular bones and dentitions)	Shell	none	Male	MA	Robust	None due to limited preservation	None due to limited preservation	174.00
33	XXIV Mesotoichia with XX, Oikopedo Axiopoulou, XXIV Mesotoichia with XX, Cremated Bones, B. -0.10		Homo 2	Cremated	PAA	Cremated to a sub-calcined degree	dry ovicaprical remains (long/short bone fragment)	none	none	Male	GA	MHOS, some form of robustness	None due to limited preservation	None due to limited preservation	66.00
40	Oikopedo Axaopoulou, Square "G", Grave XXIVb, From B+/- 0.00 Bones, 1/8/78		Homo 3	Cremated	CPAA	Cremated to a sub-calcined degree	dry faunal remains (several long/short tubular bone fragments ovicaprical in size)	Rock	none	Male	GA	Robust, MHOS	None due to limited preservation	None due to limited preservation	486.00
40a	Oikopedo Axaopoulou, Square "G", Grave XXIVb, From B+/- 0.00 Bones, 1/8/78		Homo 4	Dry	CPApp		none	none	none	Indeterminate	IN I	None observed	CPo	None observed	
34	Oik. Axiopoulou 28/7/78, Grave 27 XXVII, bones found in pithos Π1			Dry	CDPAA	—	none	none	none	Indeterminate	SA	None due to limited preservation	DP, CPo, CP	CT	
34a	Oik. Kambysi 3/8/78 Tafros ζτ, burial XXXV, bones of the 35 skeleton in the talou			Dry	CPAA	—	none	none	none	Male	LAM	None observed	CPo, OA	PCT	
36	Oik. Axiopoulou, burial ground, 11 grave XI			Cremated	C (and possible PApp)	Cremated to a sub-calcined degree	dry faunal remains (some small fragments and one large fragment possibly of an ovicaprical individual)	Shell fragment	Ceramic fragment and a prehistoric obsidian flake	Indeterminate	GA	None due to limited preservation	None due to limited preservation	None due to limited preservation	13.00
37	Oik. Axoupolou, Burial Ground, 8/7/78, Tafros A, Square Γ, Δ3, Grave XIβ, bones and charcoal within Π3						6 dry faunal bone fragments (1 larger fragment was ovicaprical in size and was not externally thick)	Three shell fragments, small piece of charcoal, and a rock	none						
38	Oik. Axiopoulou, burial ground, Square 1, 20/7/78, ----						dry faunal remains (one large tooth fragment most probably of a canid)	Carbonized shell	Piece of iron (possibly a nail fragment or iron artifact)						17.00

Plithos – Naxos Geometric Period Burial Ground Anthropology Report

#	ID / Location				Dry	PApp	—	Description	Other 1	Other 2	Sex				Value
39	13/9/78, Section of depth -0.60, bones of ~~~							dry faunal remains most probably of a bovid (distal tibial fragment, 1 rib fragment, 2 mending pieces of the mandible (possibly the left side), 2 and a half teeth in situ, and 1 tooth ex situ)	none					None observed	
41	Oik. Kambysi Π1, bones							dentitions, tubular long bone, scapular, and vertebral fragments of large mammalian (cow) and ovicaprical dry	none	none	Female	YAMA	None observed	None observed	
42	Oik. B. Axoupolou, Burial Ground, (section in pipeline) XS, 14/9/77							dry bovid bone fragment	none	none					99.00
43	Oik. Axoupoulou, Grave XXIV β, Depth -0.90, charcoal and 24b bones, 1/8/78							about 10 dry faunal fragments "There were no bones, unlike what was indicated in tag"	Wood/charcoal of a olive tree	none					
44	Oik. Kambysi Π1, bones							dry bovid remains (dental, postcranial axial and appendicular bone fragments, a horn-core fragment showing its base) - young individual based on dental wear	none	none					
46	15/7/78, Tafros A, Square B, recovered from the ~~~, charcoal							none	Several small pieces of charcoal	none					3.00
47	28/7/78, Square Δ, ~~~ Depth 30 0.02, ~~~, Burial XXX							none	Conglomerate lumps with sediment	Two bronze lumps with cupric acid					30.00
48	Oik. Axoupoulou Γ., bones, 24 Grave XXIV, 26/7/78							dry hog and ovicaprical remains (dental and postcranial fragments), dry Capra remains (2 horn-core fragments), and dry faunal fragments from a hare sized and bovid (or Sus) individual (such as a humerus)	none	Pottery fragments					
49	Oik. Axoupoulou 29/7/78, Tafos 12 XΙΙ, bones, depth +0.38 → +0.25							dry bovid remains (rib fragment) and dry ovicaprical remains (1 dentition with calculus deposit and long/short tubular bone fragments)	Rock fragment	none					90.00

#	Location	State	PApp	Description 1	Description 2	Associated	Sex	MA	MHOS	Path1	Path2	Weight
51	Oik. Kambysi Π1, faunal bones, 10/11/86	Dry		—(distal L. humeral fragment)	dry bovid and ovicaprical remains (mostly postcranial bones with mechanical cut marks)	none	none				None observed	
52	Oik. Kambysi, 22/8/78, NA T₂₈ Tafos LII, faunal bones				dry canid remains (cranial vault and 2 hemispheres of lower jaws (of same jaw) with some teeth in situ) and several long tubular bones and vertebrae of larger size also represented	none	Female	MA	MHOS	None observed	None observed	75.00
53	Oik. Axoupoulou, Square E, Grave XV, faunal bones ——				dry faunal remains (4 fragments, 1 of which was mandibular and another was a rib, 1 unidentifiable fragment had red staining) and dry Sus remains (jaw fragment)	none	none					
54	Oik. Axiopoulou plithos, Square E - a burial XVI, bones within amphora	Cremated	CDPAA	Cremated to a sub-calcined degree	tubular long bone fragment of dry faunal	none	none	Male	LA	Not Robust, MHOS	PD, CPo, OA, SP, PCP	SN	1337.00
55	Oik. Axoupoulou, Burial Ground, Square Γ', on Γ / Depth +.074, 21/7/78				dry ovicaprical remains (mandible fragment) and the talus (astragalus), calcaneus, and a rib fragment of a larger, bovid-sized individual	none	none					
56	Square β, taf. XXV, burial ground, charcoal, oik. axiopoulou	Cremated	C	Cremated to a sub-calcined degree	dry faunal remains (one long tubular bone fragment of Sus sized individual)	One small shell	Ceramic fragment	Male	GA	None due to limited preservation	None due to limited preservation	None due to limited preservation	14.00
57	Oik. Kambysi, 20/8/78, Tafros 2, Grave XLI, bones of the pyre around π3				5 dry faunal fragments of large sized individual (long/short tubular bone fragments and 2 fragments of a jaw with 1 tooth in situ) - one of the larger fragments contained reddish staining	Rock	none						115.00
58	Oik. Axoupoulou, 1/9/78, Square Δ, "Grave" XXIII, Depth -0.90, faunal bones of the jaw				dry faunal remains (jaw with 3 teeth in situ)	none	none						21.00
59	Oik. Axoupoulou, 6/9/78, Square Γ', Grave LXI, faunal remains				dry canid remains (1 jaw fragment with canine in situ)	none	none						4.00
60	Oik. Axoupoulou, 9/9/78, Square Γ', Grave XXXIV, part of animal jaw beside the urn π1				dry ovicaprical remains (jaw fragment with 4 teeth in situ)	none	none						16.00

61	Oik. Axoupoulou, 9/9/78, Grave 63 LXIII, bones, Depth -.024	6 dry faunal fragments of medium sized individual (long/short tubular bone fragments, one of which was a metacarpal/tarsal fragment)	none	127.00
62	Oik. Kambysi, 9/10/86, π2 - faunal bones	14 dry faunal bone fragments (a dentition, rib, scapula, and long/short tubular bones) - some of the short and long tubular bones had butchering cut marks	none	161.00
63	Oik. Kambysi, π3, bones	6 dry bovid sized faunal remains (jaw fragments, long tubular bones, and 1 tooth ex situ)	none	67.00
64	Oik. Kambysi, embankment, (No other data given)	dry faunal remains (2 dry faunal long tubular bones, 1 of which had cupric acid staining and was cut and shaved perfectly, showing that it was manipulated, which may indicate that it was an artifact)	none	221.00
65	Oik. Kambysi π1, faunal bones, 10/11/86	dry faunal remains of a large sized/bovid sized individual (9 fragments, all of which were long/short tubular bone fragments)	none	272.00
66	Oik. Kambysi, 13/11/86, π,, bones	2 dry faunal fragments of a smaller individual	none	8.00
67	Oik. Kambysi, 9/10/86, π1, bones	dry faunal bone fragment (large calcaneous) of Sus sized or larger (i.e. bovid) with some butchering cut marks present	none	71.00
68	Oik. Kambysi, embankment, bones	8 dry faunal fragments (long/short tubular and flat bone fragments) of large individuals (up to bovid size and smaller)	none	48.00

#	Location			Condition	Analyst	Description	Bone	Other	Sex	Age	Robusticity/Pathology	Notes	Count
69	Oik. Kambysi, without indication, bones					2 dry faunal fragments of a medium sized individual (1 fragment from a tubular long bone and 1 from the pelvic area)	none	none					42.00
70	Oik. Kambysi on the outside, Grave 2, for 'Av. π4, bones					3 dry faunal fragments (1 long tubular bone and 2 from the jaw with cut marks (dressing) on both jaw fragments) of a Sus to bovid sized individual	none	Ceramic fragment					82.00
71	Oik. Kambysi π1					dry remains of a possibly ovicaprical (long bone tubular fragment, which was an epiphysis of a medium sized individual [ovicaprical humeral distal ½])	none	none					8.00
72	Oik. Kambysi, 17/11/1986, π5, bones					dry faunal remains of a larger individual (a flat bone fragment)	none	none					36.00
73	Oik. Kambysi, 19/11/86, π2, bones, horns, and faunal dentition					10 dry fragments of a large faunal individual (4 fragments of horn-core, long/short tubular bone fragments, and 2 dentitions. The horn-core fragments were sharp and angular as those of Capra, with a visible base)	none	none					343.00
74	Oik. Kambysi, 10/10/86, π1, bones					14 larger fragments and a few small bone flakes of a larger dry faunal individual (long/short tubular bone fragments with butchering cut marks)	none	none					379.00
75	oikopedo kambysi π1, bones		Dry	PAA	—	dry large collection of CDPAA remains possibly from Sus, bovid, and ovicaprical individuals	none	none	Female	GA	Not Robust, MHOS	OA	
76	Oik. Kambysi 8/10/86, π3, bones					3 dry faunal fragments of a larger sized (bovid) individual (1 rib of larger size and 1 long/short tubular bone fragment that had butchering cut marks)	none	none				PCT	37.00

#	Location/Description			Faunal remains		Other finds					Weight (g)
77	Oik. Kambysi, 17/11/1986, n7 bones			2 dry remains of medium sized faunal (1 long/short tubular bone and 1 fragment from the jaw with cut marks)	none	none					25.00
78	Oik. Kambysi, 21/8/87, O1, bones of Northeast --assuming T6, depth 1.70			11 fragments of larger mammalian individual	none	none					152.00
79	faunal bones and shells			dry remains of large faunal (i.e. bovid) (left mandibular fragment, 5 ribs, and 8 long/short tubular bones)	Four shells	none					166.00
80	Oik. Kambysi, faunal bones			4 dry fragments of a larger sized faunal (i.e. bovid) (3 long tubular bone fragments, and 1 rib)	none	none					107.00
81	Oik. Kambysi, 18/8/1978, M2 pieces of iron from section A, 4 grave 4, depth: 0.45-0.55			dry faunal remains of at least 2 different species, Sus and ovicaprical. Ovicaprical individual represented by a dentition ex situ. Sus individual represented by jaw fragments with 2 dentitions in situ. Other dry faunal remains were vertebra, ribs, about 13 long/short tubular bone fragments and possible fragment of the ear (acousticus).	none	Two pottery sherds					275.00
82	19/11/86, n4, animal bones, Oik. Kambysi	Dry	PApp	5 dry faunal fragments of a larger individual	---	none	Female	GA	None observed	None observed	None observed
83	Oik. Kambysi, 9/10/86, n2, bones			~56 dry faunal fragments of bovid individual (2 dentitions ex situ, long/short tubular bones and other various flat bone fragments) and ovicaprical individual (long/short tubular bone fragments and a horn-core fragment)	none	none					>1200.00

84	Oik. Kambysi, 10/8/87, O1, faunal pieces of a section between T5 and T8, Depth 1.80 and 2.0, B, section of T8			dry faunal remains of bovid individual (1 dentition ex situ, talus, flat bone fragments, and long tubular bone fragments with butchering cut marks) and ovicaprical individual (fragments of the jaw with dentitions ex situ, short/long bone fragments, flat bone fragments, and ~3 fragments of horn-core)	Two rocks	Three ceramic fragments, one of larger size		1500.00
85	Oik. Zafeiropoulou, 28/9/87, O1, bones			20 dry fragments of a bovid individual (1 tooth ex situ, showing wear which indicates an older individual, a rib fragment, flat bone fragment, and other unidentified fragments) and another smaller ovicaprical individual (several rib fragments, flat bone fragments, long/short tubular bone fragments, and other unidentified fragments)	none	none		237.00
86	Oik. Zafeiropoulou, 18/9/87, Π4 of the well, faunal bones + horns			dry faunal remains (1 dentition ex situ from a bovid with considerable wear, indicating an older individual, and a horn-core from a Capra that was broken off [not cut mechsnically] showing the hollow base. Other remains included fragments of the jaw, ribs, short/long tubular bone fragments and other flat bone fragments)	Rock	none		155.00

87			Oik. Zafeiropoulou, 18/9/87, Π4 of the well, faunal bones + horns					dry faunal remains of a Capra (5 horn-core fragments that were all broken off in a way indicating that it was not by butchering), an Ovis individual (1 horn-core), and a bovid individual (jaw fragment with 2 dentitions in situ and 1 ex situ which revealed wear). Other dry faunal remains included rib fragments (1 shows cut marks), and other long/short tubular bone fragments.	none				none
88			Oik. Zafeiropoulou, Ο1					dry remains of a Capra individual (6 horn-core fragments broken off [not butchered] showing the hollow base), an Sus individual (1 jaw fragment with 2 dentitions and roots in situ), an ovicaprical individual (1 jaw fragment with 2 dentitions in situ and an acetabulum), and a bovid sized individual (long/short tubular bone fragments, talus, and a vertebral fragment [unossified indicating a younger individual])	none				>1500.00

#	Context	Description	Matrix	Weight (g)
89	Oik. Zafeiropoulou, 16/9/87, O1 of the well	dry faunal remains including Capra (2 horn-core fragments- broken off and showed hollow bases), Ovis/ram (1 horn-core fragment cut mechanically with no hollow base showing), bovid (1 jaw fragment with 1 dentition [worn down] in situ, 5 horn-core fragments [1 from a younger individual]- broken off and showed hollow bases. 2 of the horn-core fragments contained cranial components) Present was a fragment of a cranium with sutures, 2 ribs with cut marks, long tubular bone fragments, flat bone fragments, and 3 dentitions ex situ, 1 of which was from a Sus and the other 2 were from a herbivore of a young age (based on lack of wear).	Conglomerates	>1500.00
90	Oik. Kambysi, 17/8/87, O1, bones of NA angle cut --- the road, Depth 1.05	dry remains of a bovid individual (long bone fragment with cut marks). Other dry faunal remains included 2 dentitions ex situ, ribs, and the vertebra of a smaller individual.	none	261.00
91	Oik. Zafeiropoulou, 17/8/87, n1 of the well, faunal horns	dry faunal remains (2 horn-core fragments, possibly of Capra individuals [hollow base unable to be seen due to preservation], and 1 other dry faunal remain of a medium sized individual)	none	65.00
92	Oik. Zafeiropoulou, well - Deposit 1, bones	14 dry faunal remains of bovid sized individual (long/short tubular bone fragments, flat bone fragments [including a rib of larger size] and other unidentifiable fragments)	none	165.00

#												
93	Oik. Zafeiropoulou, 8/10/87, п3, faunal bones and horns					dry faunal remains of a smaller individual (long/short tubular bone fragments, flat bone fragments, and a jaw fragment), Capra individual (horn-core fragment), and a bovid individual (the glenoid cavity)	none					230.00
94	Oiko. Melissourgou, center of burial ground, 23/10/2002, Square 3B - tal 14, depth 3.40 #593			Dry	CDPAA	—	none	Female	SAYA	MHOS	DP, PD, CPo	PCT
95	Oik. Vatrakokili, 14/8/87, O1, bones of Δ. ~~~ T$_{ss}$, in northeast cut of the site					dry faunal remains (long/short tubular bone fragments and other various bone fragments)	none					16.00
96	Oik. Zafeiropoulou, 17/8/87, п1 of the well, processed bone 'flute'					2 dry faunal long/short tubular bone fragments, 1 with butchering cut marks and the other was a fragment of a flute.	Long/short tubular faunal bone fragment from a flute (polished and cut mechanically)					
97	Oik. Zafeiropoulou, 20/8/87, O1 embankment					9 dry bone fragments which represented at least 2 different species. Present was 1 dentition ex situ that was missing the crown, long/short tubular bone fragments, flat bone fragments, and other various bone fragments.	Ceramic fragment					184.00
98	Oik. Zafeiropoulou, 16/9/87, п$_2$ of the well, bones					18 dry faunal fragments (a cranial fragment with sutures, rib fragments, long/short tubular bone fragments, flat bone fragments, and the base of a horn-core)	none					350.00

#												
99	Oik. Zafeiropoulou 21/9/87, n, cf the well, faunal bones and horns						6 horn-cores included 1 that is sharp, twisted, and triangular-like, 2 that are round (possibly small bovid), and 1 that had a cranial component with it. Present were bovid remains. 1 jaw fragment from a bovid had 2 dentitions in situ and 1 ex situ with considerable wear. 1 jaw fragment of a medium sized faunal individual had 1 dentition in situ and other roots in situ. Other remains included a larger rib, flat bone fragments, long/short tubular bone, 1 of which shows cut marks	none			>1200.00	
100	Oik. Zafeiropoulou, 18/9/87, Π4 of the well, faunal bones and horns						dry Capra remains (3 triangular and sharp horn-core fragments - 2 horn-core fragments broken off with hollow base showing [not mechanical/butcher marks] and 3rd fragment shows cut marks) and dry Bovid remains (3 dentitions ex situ [considerable wear]) Also present were long/short bone fragments (1 showing cut marks) and flat bone fragments.	One marine shell				
101	Oik. Zafeiropoulou, 14/9/87, n₂						5 dry faunal fragments of medium sized individual, all seeming to be from the jaw. 1 fragment had 1 tooth in situ.	none			99.00	
102	Oik. Zafeiropoulou, 17/9/87, n₂ (section A well), faunal horn						1 dry faunal (possibly ovicaprical) remain (a fragment of a horn-core)	none			23.00	

103	Oik. Zafeiropoulou, 18/8/87, O₂, bones of pithos					dry faunal remains of at least 2 different species, 1 large and 1 small (long/short tubular bones with slight cut marks, ribs, and other flat bone fragments)	none				120.00
104	Oik. Zafeiropoulou, well - Deposit 1, bones					2 dry small Capra remains (horn-core fragments) and dry faunal remains (flat bone fragments and 1 cranial fragment)	none				41.00
105	Oik. Zafeiropoulou, 18/9/87, Π, of the well, faunal bones and horns					dry Capra remains (horn-core fragment) dry faunal remains (1 horn-core with cranial component, 1 horn-core likely of a younger ram, jaw fragment, and tubular bone fragment) dry bovid remains (a left calcaneus)	none				200.00
106	Oik. Zafeiropoulou, 22/9/81, Π, of the well, bones					dry Ovis remains (4 horn-core fragments broken off so hollow base showing) and dry faunal remains (4 flat bones and a long/short bone fragment)	none				280.00
107	Oik. Zafeiropoulou, 19/8/87, O₂					12 fragments of at least 2 different species which were ovicaprical in size (one larger that the other), ribs, long/short tubular bone fragments, and a femoral or humeral head of an ovicaprical individual	none				73.00
108	Oik. Kambysi, 19/8/87, O₂ bones of the southeast site cut, Depth 1.05 of ~- Road A.					22 dry faunal fragments (cranial fragments, a jaw fragment, a long/short tubular bone fragment [with cut marks], flat bone fragments, and articular surfaces)	Two rocks	Three ceramic pieces			85.00

109	Oik. Kambysi, 24/8/87, O, bones of ~~~ B. ~~~ Grave 1, Depth 2.10 of northeast site cut		dry bovid remains (a large ulna fragment) and dry faunal remains (herbivorous tooth ex situ, a jaw fragment, flat bone fragment, long/short tubular bones [1 long/short tubular bone fragment from a smaller animal had cut marks], and a rib fragment from a small individual)	none	Two small ceramic fragments	250.00
110	Oik. Zafeiropoulou, 19/8/87, O₁		dry faunal remains of at least 2 different species, 1 of which was ovicaprical (3 fragments of jaws [1 with 3 teeth in situ, another with 2 teeth in situ, and a 3rd with 1 tooth in situ], 5 fragments of teeth ex situ, ribs, and long/short tubular bones)	none	Ceramic fragment	487.00
111	Oik. Pantelaiou, 28/8/87, O₆ (~~~), H/8 - 2/5		dry bovid remains (1 large probable pelvic fragment, 1 rib fragment, 1 flat bone fragment, and long/short tubular bone fragments [1 long tubular fragment was mechanically cut and another contained iron staining]) Both of these long tubular fragments contained floral roots on the bone.	none	none	280.00
112	Oik. Zafeiropoulou, 48/9/87, n₄ (well deposit 1) bones		dry bovid remains (long tubular bone), dry ovicaprical remains (a long/short tubular bone and 1 unossified fragment of a vertebra, indicating a younger individual), and dry faunal remains (flat bone and long/short tubular bone fragments)	none	none	318.00

Plithos - Naxos Geometric Period Burial Ground Anthropology Report

#	Location/ID					Description			Sex	SAYA	MHOS	Pathology	Notes	Value
113	Oik. Kambysi, 18/8/87, O₁, bones of ---- Τ₈, Depth 1-1.8					~33 dry faunal fragments of at least 2 different species, 1 larger and 1 smaller (1 horn-core fragment most likely Ovis in nature [broken off so the hollow base was showing-not mechanically cut], piece of jaw with 2 teeth in situ, rib fragments [of 2 different sizes], flat bone fragments, and long/short tubular bone fragments)			none	none				421.00
114	Oik. Bas. Melissourgou center of burial ground 27/8/2022 Space 3B/3Γ - Τaf 7, depth 2.95μ #357, 7 bones				Dry	CPAA	—		none	none	Probable Female	SAYA	MHOS	None due to limited preservation	None due to limited preservation
115	Oik. Zafeiropoulou, 1/9/87, Π₃ ---- pipeline 2, bones					8 fragments of at least 2 different species, 1 of which was ovicaprical (unossified vertebral fragment which indicated a younger individual) and the other of a larger species (horn-core fragment possibly of a Capra, scapula fragment, an epiphyseal plate from a vertebra, and other long/short bone fragments [1 of which shows depressions/cut marks])			none	none					108.00
116	Oik. Zafeiropoulou, Π₁ (well deposit), bones					7 dry faunal bone fragments (a cranial fragment with sutures [of a young individual and very porous], long tubular bone fragments with slight cut marks, and flat bone fragments) and dry bovid remains (rib)			none	none					222.00
117	Oik. Zafeiropoulou, well deposit 1, (----) bones					3 faunal bone fragments. Present was 1 horn-core fragment and 2 long tubular bone fragments, which represented a larger individual.			none	none					72.00
118	Oik. Zafeiropoulou, 16/9/87, Π₂ (of the well) bones					4 dry bovid bone fragments. 1 fragment had deep cut marks.			none	none					222.00

119	Oik. Zafeiropoulou, 28/9/87, Τμ. bones					5 dry faunal bone fragments, all of which were long/short tubular bone fragments of medium sized individual. 2 long/short tubular bone fragments showed slight cut marks.	none	none	127.00
120	Oik. Pantelaiou, 24/8/87, Πμ. -/m-1/3, processed bone					dry faunal remains including a talus (ovicaprical with darker patina as if handled by hand) of a small individual and 1 long bone fragment.	none	none	9.00
121	Oik. Zafeiropoulou, 17/9/87, Π.- (section A well), bones					5 dry faunal bone fragments (1 long tubular bone fragment and 4 cranial fragments [with 1 seeming to be from the area of the acousticus] - 2 of the cranial fragments showed unossification, indicating a younger individual)	none	none	36.00
122	Oik. Zafeiropoulou, well-deposit faunal bones and horns					11 dry faunal bone fragments. A long tubular bone of a bovid sized individual showing deep cut marks was present. 5 horn-core fragments of a possible Capra were represented [1 broken off in non-mechanical way showing hollow base]. Other fragments included a rib and other flat bones fragments.	none	none	193.00

123		Oik. Zafeiropoulou, 22/9/87, Π, (well-deposit 1) faunal bones and horns							dry Ovis remains (1 horn-core fragment), dry Capra remains (1 horn-core fragment. Both horn-core fragments broken off (not mechanically) so that the hollow base was showing) and dry faunal remains (a cranial component showing acoustic pore and sutures, a long tubular bone fragment [of a medium sized individual], and 1 flat bone fragment)	none		370.00
124		Oik. Zafeiropoulou, well, deposit 1, faunal horn							dry faunal remains of a younger possible Capra (1 horn-core fragment possibly cut off mechanically in a rough way)	none		23.00
125		Oik. Zafeiropoulou, 17/9/87, Π, (of the well), faunal bones							18 dry faunal remains (an unfused vertebral fragment, an unfused scapular fragment, other flat bone fragments, long/short tubular bone fragments, and a larger tarsal fragment present) Also present were 4 fragments of horn-core. A bovid individual was represented by rib and long bone fragments. A medium sized individual was also represented.	none		494.00

#											
126	Oik. Zafeiropoulou, 21/9/87, Γ₃ (of the well), faunal horns					dry Capra remains (10 horn-core fragments with few cut marks) and dry Ovis remains (2 horn-core fragments with excavation trauma and marks even older than the excavation trauma). Also, present were 3 smaller fragments of horn-core and 1 cranial fragment with sutures. All of the horn-core fragments were broken off non-mechanically showing the hollow base.	none	none			>1200.00
127	Oik. Zafeiropoulou, 1/9/87, Π₁ (Δ. pipeline '2) bones					6 dry faunal bone fragments of a medium sized individual (long/short tubular bone fragments and irregular bone fragments- few cut marks present)	none	none			179.00
128	Oik. Zafeiropoulou, 7/9/87, O₁ (-·-- A of T₂)					dry Capra remains (3 horn-core fragments, all showing their hollow bases. The smallest one was of a younger individual which showed cut marks and the largest one was cut mechanically at the tip) and dry Sus remains (a left mandibular Sus fragment with 3 teeth in situ), dry bovid remains (long tubular bone fragments and rib fragments), and dry faunal remains (long/short tubular fragments and flat bone fragments)	none	none			>1200.00
129	Oik. Bas. Melissourgou Center of Burial Ground - Square 2B, E4 depth 2.25u #336, bones			Cremated	CDPAA	Well cremated to a calcined degree	thermally altered faunal bone fragments	Pottery flakes	Male	YAMA	Robust, MHOS	SP, CPo	none observed	816.00
130	Oik. Zafeiropoulou, 2/10/87, O₁, bones					5 dry faunal bone fragments of a medium sized individual. All of the remains were long/short tubular bone fragments, with one showing cut marks.	none	none			86.00

131	1/9/87, Π₂ (of the section ~~~) ~~3, bones	5 dry faunal bone fragments (fragments of a jaw, 2 long tubular bones, and 2 unidentified fragments)	none	54.00
132	Zafeiropoulou, 2/10/1987, Π₃, bones	At least 2 different species were represented; 1 of medium size (3 rib fragments) and 1 of a smaller size (rib fragment). Other remains included long/short tubular bone fragments and flat bone fragments.	none	56.00
133	23/9/87, Zaf. Π, (section ~~~ B. section) bones	6 faunal bone fragments of a medium sized individual (a rib fragment with cut marks, 1 flat bone fragment, 1 long tubular fragment, and 3 irregular bone fragments)	none	95.00
134	Zaf. 10/9/87, Π, bones/horns	dry faunal remains included 2 fragments of horn-core, 1 of which was Capra and had cut marks. A bovid individual was represented by long tubular bone fragments, ribs, and 1 dentition ex situ showing considerable wear. Other dry faunal remains included long tubular bone fragments (1 with cut marks), rib fragments, flat bone fragments, and other unidentifiable bone fragments.	One nail and one ceramic fragment	500.00
135	Oik. Zafeiropoulou, 22/9/87, Π, (of the well), faunal bones	18 dry faunal bone fragments including 3 Capra horn-core fragments. A bovid individual was represented by long tubular bone fragments. Other remains included a tooth fragment ex situ, long/short tubular bone fragments, and flat bone fragments.	none	~500.00

#	Location/Date	Description	Notes	Value
136	Zafeiropoulou, 17/8/87, n₃, bones	8 faunal bone fragments including 2 jaw fragments, 1 of which was from a Sus and had 2 dentitions in situ. A bovid individual was represented by a rib fragment. Other remains included long/short tubular and flat bone fragments.	none	38.00
137	Zafeiropoulou, 11/9/87, n₁ (---2), bones	4 dry faunal fragments of a medium sized individual. Also, present were 2 long/short tubular bone fragments, 1 rib, and 1 articular surface.	none	35.00
138	Zafeiropoulou, n₁, of BA ~~~ site, bones	6 dry faunal bone fragments of at least 2 species. An Ovicaprical individual was represented by a long tubular bone fragment. A larger sized individual was represented by an ulna fragment. Other remains included a flat bone fragment with butchering cut marks (from a larger individual) and long/short tubular bone fragments.	none	122.00
139	Oik. Zafeiropoulou, 23/9/87, n₂ ~~~	2 dry faunal remains, 1 of a larger individual and 1 of a smaller individual. Both fragments were from long/short tubular bones.	none	58.00
140	Oik. Zafeiropoulou, 30/9/87, n₂, bones	10 faunal bone fragments of at least 2 different species, 1 of which was bovid and the other was a smaller sized species. Other dry faunal remains included long/short tubular bone fragments and 2 small unidentified fragments.	none	148.00

#	Location			Description		Finds					
141	Oik. Zafeiropoulou, 1/9/87, Ο, Δ pipeline 2			8 jaw fragments. 4 of these jaw fragments have teeth in situ, and of these 4, 1 was of a bovid. 2 jaw fragments have dentitions ex situ, and of these 2, 1 was of a bovid. Present were 2 horn-core fragments with 1 broken off (non-mechanically) so the hollow base was shown. Other remains included at least 7 fragments of the cranium, flat bone fragments, and long tubular bone fragments. 1 of the long tubular bone fragments indicated a younger individual and 1 was mechanically cut. The bovid jaw showed evidence of a cut mark.	none	Ceramic flake					506.00
142	Oik. Zafeiropoulou, 17/8/87, Π, bones			5 dry faunal bone fragments including 2 mending horn-core fragments with cranial components attached (seemed to be from an Ovis individual). There were also 2 long tubular bone fragments and 1 unidentifiable fragment.	none	none					107.00
143	Oik. Zafeiropoulou, 25/8/87, between amphora k' T, bones			2 dry faunal bone fragments, 1 of which was a flat bone and the other was a long tubular bone.	none	none					8.00
144	Oikopedo Bas. Melissourgou, Plithos-Chora, 9-8-2002, Square 1B / Grave, Depth, 2.60-2.95m #274	Dry	CPApp	dry ovicaprical horn core, tubular frags, and Sus dentitions			Female	MA	Femoral MHOS	None observed	None observed

#	Provenance	Notes	Homo	Condition	Class	Description	Associated	Finds	Sex	Age	Robustness	Observations 1	Observations 2	Weight
145	Oik. Bas. Melissourgou, Taf. 1		Homo 1	Cremated	CPAA	cremated (6 long/short tubular thermally altered bone fragments (various bone fragments of smaller faunal and 3 dentitions ex situ and 1 dentition in situ with jaw component, ribs and long/short tubular bone fragments)	none	none	Male	YA	V. Robust, MHOS	None observed	None observed	380.00
145a			Homo 2	Dry	PApp	Ranged from thermally altered to sub-calcined —(L. and R. femoral fragments)	none	none	Female	GA	None observed due to limiting preservation	None observed	None observed	
146	Oikopedo Bas. Melissourgou, Square 2"G"-Taf.8, Depth.- 2.80m, #370, Bones	Included an additional HomoDRY, a permanent mandibular premolar, ~15y, indeterminate sex		Dry	PApp	(long bone fragments)	tooth of an herbivore	none	Indeterminate	IN II (8-9y.)	None observed	None observed	None observed	
147	Oik. Bas. Melissourgoy, Square 1"G", From Vase within Taf. 9, from #371, 28/8/2002; and from Square 1"G", Notia Pareia, Depth. 2.15-2.45, #375, 28/8/2002	Included an additional Homo DRY, a permanent dry Left mandibular incisor, ~45 (LAMA), indeterminate sex		Cremated	CDPAA	Well cremated to a sub-calcined degree	dry faunal bone fragment	Two roots, charcoal and a shell	Male	LA	Robust, MHOS	OA, SP, CPo, PD	SN	641 & 322->963.00
153	Oik. Zafeiropoulou, 6/10/78, O$_2$						dry faunal remains of an individual that was ovicaprical in size. The remains included 3 jaw fragments with teeth in situ, 2 teeth ex situ, an orbital fragment, scapula fragments, other flat bone fragments, and long tubular bone fragments (1 with cut marks).	none						432.00

156	Oik. Zafeiropoulou, O₂, 13/10/87			dry faunal remains (4 Capra horn-cores, a cranial component, ribs, and flat bones)	none		416.00
157	Oik. Zafeiropoulou, 13/10/1987, O₂			dry faunal remains of at least 2 different species, ovicaprical and bovid (2 horn-core fragments [Capra in nature] and other dry faunal remains included a tooth ex situ, various flat bone fragments, ribs, long/short tubular bone fragments, and other unidentifiable fragments.	Two shells	none	427.00
158	Oik. Zafeiropoulou, O₃			12 dry faunal bone fragments including 1 Capra horn-core, flat bone fragments, long/short tubular bone fragments, and other unidentifiable fragments.	none		108.00
159	Zafeiropoulou, O₃			dry faunal remains of at least 3 different species, most likely ovicaprical, Sus and bovid. Dry faunal remains included 6 dentitions ex situ - 1 of the dentitions was a canine from a Sus. Also, present were cranial components, ribs (large and small, showing the presence of more than 1 species), flat bone fragments, and long/short tubular bone fragments (few showing butchering cut marks).	none	Ceramic fragment	794.00
160	Oik. Zafeiropoulou, O₃			dry faunal remains of at least 2 different species, 1 of a medium size and 1 of a smaller size (2 Capra horn-cores, a cranial component, a jaw fragment with 3 teeth in situ, rib fragments, flat bone fragments, and long/short tubular	none	Ceramic fragment	375.00

161	Oik. Zafeiropoulou O₃	6 dry faunal bone fragments seeming to be from a bovid individual (1 larger jaw fragment with partial dentition in situ, 2 other smaller jaw fragments "maid?" with the larger, and 4 long/short tubular fragments.	none	275.00
162	Oik. Zafeiropoulou O₃	dry faunal remains (3 Capra horn-core fragments, a large mandibular fragment of a bovid individual, long/short tubular bone fragments, rib fragments, and 3 other jaw fragments)	none	602.00
163	Oik. Zafeiropoulou O₃	12 faunal bone fragments of at least 2 different species, medium in size and smaller in size (rib fragments, long/short tubular bone fragments, and 2 irregular bone fragments)	none	362.00
164	Oik. Zafeiropoulou O₃	dry faunal remains of at least 2 different species (1 Capra horn-core fragment showing hollow base, 2 ribs of a bovid, flat bone fragments, and long/short tubular bone fragments)	none	444.00
165	Oik. Zafeiropoulou O₃	dry faunal remains of at least 2 different species, medium in size and smaller in size (3 teeth ex situ, 1 vertebral fragment, flat bone fragments, long/short tubular bone fragments, and 1 articular surface fragment)	Marine shell	226.00
166	Oik. Zafeiropoulou O₃	11 dry faunal bone fragments of at least 2 different species, 1 of a larger size and 1 of a smaller size (ribs, a flat bone with cut marks, long/short tubular bone fragments, and other unidentifiable bone fragments)	none	393.00

167	Oik. Zafeiropoulou O₂					12 dry faunal bone fragments of a medium sized individual (2 mending jaw fragments with 3 teeth in situ, ribs, flat bones fragments, and long/short tubular bone fragments)	none	210.00
168	Oik. Zafeiropoulou O₂					17 dry faunal bone fragments of at least 2 different species, bovid (rib fragment) and ovicaprical in size. Other dry faunal remains included 1 jaw fragment (with 1 tooth in situ) and 3 teeth ex situ (2 of which represented a different species). Also, present were ribs, flat bone fragments, and long/short tubular bone fragments.	none	101.00
169	Oik. Zafeiropoulou 1/10/1987, O₁					dry faunal remains of individual that was ovicaprical in size (long/short tubular bone fragments)	none	
170	Oik. Zafeiropoulou 9/10/1987, O₁					dry bone and dental fragments of an herbivore (could be ovicaprical) and dry Sus faunal remains	none	
171	Oik. Zafeiropoulou O₁					22 dry faunal bone fragments of at least 2 species (3 Capra horn-cores, 2 ribs, long/short tubular bone fragments, unidentified bone fragments, 1 tooth ex situ of a larger individual, and 1 jaw fragment with a tooth in situ of a smaller individual)	Rock	240.00
172	Oikopedo Zafeiropoulou, 26/8/1987, O, bones of taf. 1, Depth 0.20-0.50					dry remains of a smaller mammalian faunal (a rib, a tooth [probably of a Sus], and tubular long bones)	none	
173	Oik. Zafeiropoulou, 1/10/1987, O₁					2 dry bone fragments of faunal-mammalian (possibly Sus).	none	

#	Context			Condition	Description		Sex	Age				Value
174	Oik. Zafeiropoulou O₃				4 dry faunal bone fragments, all of which were long/short tubular bone fragments. There were at least 2 individuals present (1 larger and 1 smaller).	none						275.00
175	Oikop. Zafeiropoulou, 28/9/87, O₄, bones				dry faunal remains of a larger mammalian, an ovicaprical, and of a smaller mammalian.	none						
176	Oikopedo Zafeiropoulou O5 28/9/87			Dry	PApp (right distal humerus, right proximal end of an ulna and the right radius)	dry remains of a bovid and an ovicaprical	none				None observed	
177	Oik. Zafeiropoulou, Π1					dry faunal remains of at least 2 different species (1 horn core fragment, at least 3 jaw fragments [1 with 3 teeth in situ and 1 with 1 tooth in situ], rib fragments, flat bone fragments, long/short tubular bone fragments, and unidentified fragments). Also, present was a vertebral fragment of a larger faunal individual.	none	Female	GA	MHOS	None observed	>1100.00
178	Oik. Zafeiropoulou, O₄					1 dry faunal fragment representing a probable humerus distal end. The individual was of larger size, probably bovid.	none					137.00
179	Oik. Zafeiropoulou Y₁					15 dry faunal bone fragments of a larger individual, possibly bovid (a possible cranial fragment, 1 jaw fragment, rib fragments, flat bone fragments, and long/short tubular bone fragments)	none					333.00
180	Oikop. Zafeiropoulou 29/9/1987 O2			Dry	PApp (humeral midshaft)	dry fragment of a mammalian faunal	none	Probable Female	GA	None observed	None observed	
181	Oik. Zafeiropoulou Π₃					12 dry faunal bone fragments, which were ovicaprical in size (2 jaw fragments, flat bones fragments, long/short tubular bones, and other unidentified fragments)	none					314.00

182	Oikopedo Zafeiropoulou, 14/10/87					3 dry faunal remains, most likely of an ovicaprical.	none				
183	Oik. Zafeiropoulou, 16/10/1987, O1					a dry bone fragment of a larger mammalian, most likely bovid.	none				
184	Oik. Zafeiropoulou, 13/10/1987, O2					a dry mammalian faunal fragment	none				
						11 dry faunal bone fragments of at least 2 different species, bovid (a long tubular bone fragment) and a smaller individual (a smaller tubular bone fragment). Also, present were rib fragments, flat bone fragments and other long/short tubular bone fragments.					363.00
185	Oik. Zafeiropoulou O2						none				
186	Oikopedo Zafeiropoulou I14, 17/8/87, bones and faunal horns					dry faunal bone and horn fragments (a horn-core of an ovicaprical with mechanical cut marks shown at its base, some other horn fragments, and a bone fragment of a bovid)	none				
187	Oik. Zafeiropoulou O.					dry Sus remains (canine tooth ex situ in 2 mending fragments) and other dry faunal remains (flat bone fragments, long/short tubular bone fragments, and 1 horn-core fragment in which you could see the hollow base)	none				328.00
188	Oik. Zafeiropoulou, 5/10/87, r2 bones					dry faunal remains included a large tooth from an herbivore, possibly a cow, that had been worn down due to mastication. A horn-core, rib, and other fragments were also represented. Butchering marks were present.	none				

189	Oik. Zafeiropoulou O₁		19 dry faunal bone fragments of at least 2 different species (a Capra horn-core fragment, 2 rib fragments, and long/short tubular bone fragments with cut marks [1 of the long bones revealed an unossified end, indicating a younger individual])	none	none	257.00
190	Oik. Zafeiropoulou, 27/8/87, Γ₁, East of T₄, Depth = 1.19, bones		5 dry faunal bone fragments (4 long bone fragments, 1 rib fragment, and 1 dentition of a bovid)	none		
191	Oik. Zafeiropoulou O₁		dry faunal remains of at least 2 different species, likely bovid and ovicaprical (cranial fragments (with sutures), 2 jaw fragments, 1 tooth ex situ missing crown, 2 vertebral fragments, various rib fragments, flat bone fragments, and long/short tubular bone fragments)	Small fragment of sediment stained with cupric acid	none	347.00
192	Oik. Zafeiropoulou 25/9/87, O₃		dry ovicaprical remains (1 unfused long bone fragment) and dry bovid remains (a long bone fragment with a butchering mark)	none	none	
193	Oik. Zafeiropoulou 16/10/1987, O₂		5 dry faunal remains (a jaw fragment, 2 ribs, a possible humerus, and a flat bone of ovicaprical size)	none	none	
194	Oik. Zafeiropoulou O₄		4 dry faunal bone fragments (1 horn-core fragment which was Capra in nature [had the hollow base showing and deep depressions/cut marks], 2 long tubular bone fragments, and 1 flat bone fragment)	none	none	55.00

195	Oik. Zafeiropoulou, 27/8/87, Π₁, East of T₄ (Depth:1.95), bones			dry faunal remains including long/short bones and a dentition of a bovid and Sus.	none	none	
196	Oik. Zafeiropoulou Π6			dry faunal remains including 3 flat bones and 1 talus of a medium sized individual.	Rock	none	46.00
197	Oik. Zafeiropoulou 23/9/87, Π₂ (~~~), faunal remains			dry faunal dental and bone fragments. The remains were from mammalian fauna such as Sus, herbivores (ovicaprical and bovid).	none	none	
198	Oik. Zafeiropoulou Π₆			5 dry faunal bone fragments (1 horn-core fragment (Capra in nature)-broken off so that the hollow base was showing, 1 rib, 1 flat bone fragment, and 2 long bone fragments)	none	none	91.00
199	Oik. Zafeiropoulou O₁			10 dry faunal fragments of a medium sized individual (5 flat bone fragments, 3 rib fragments, and 2 long/short tubular bone fragments)	none	none	44.00
200	Oik. Zafeiropoulou, 8/9/87, Π2, bones			3 dry faunal bone fragments. A cranial, short bone, and flat bone were represented from an ovicaprical sized individual. 2 of the fragments were unfused.	none	none	
201	Oik. Zafeiropoulou O₂			2 dry faunal bone fragments (1 partial horn-core with a cranial component attached and a small cranial fragment)	none	none	25.00
202	Oik. Zafeiropoulou, 13/10/1987, O₃			dry faunal remains included a mandible of an ovicaprical with dentitions in situ and a rib fragment.	none	none	

						134.00
						285.00
						48.00
					none	
					none	
					none	
					none	
					none	
					Rock	
					none	
	dry faunal remains included 5 mandibular fragments of an ovicaprical faunal with teeth in situ. Also represented were some tubular long bones and rib fragments of an ovicaprical and a smaller mammalian sized faunal.	dry faunal remains (9 horn-core fragments [possibly from a Capra individual] and 1 tooth ex situ)	dry faunal remains of what was most likely a canid and a larger mammalian faunal. The canid was represented by 2 tibiae, 1 femur, 2 rib fragments, and a left mandible with teeth in situ, while the larger mammalian was represented by a phalanga.	25 faunal bone fragments of at least 2 different species were represented, ovicaprical and a larger individual (1 tooth ex situ [herbivorous in nature], rib fragments, flat bone fragments, and long/short tubular bone fragments)	3 dry faunal bone fragments included 1 bone fragment that was unfused. They seemed to be of an individual that was ovicaprical in size.	2 dry faunal fragments (1 Capra horn-core fragment showing its hollow base and a jaw fragment of a larger individual)
	Oik. Zafeiropoulou 18/9/87, π₁ (of the ---)	Oik. Zafeiropoulou O₁	Oik. Zafeiropoulou, 7/10/87, O₂	Oik. Zafeiropoulou π₂	Oik. Zafeiropoulou, 23/9/87, π₁ (section --- South section)	Oik. Zafeiropoulou π₄
203	204	205	206	207	208	

Plithos - Naxos Geometric Period Burial Ground Anthropology Report

ID	Context				Condition	Side	Description		Sex	Age	Pathology		Measurement
209	Oik. Zafeiropoulou, 6/10/87, π. - faunal bones						5 dry faunal fragments that appeared to belong to bovid and ovicaprical sized fauna.	none					
210	Oik. Zafeiropoulou, 28/8/87, π₂, space between T6, pipeline 2 k pipeline 1, Depth: 1.10-1.35, bones						dry faunal bone fragments included an assortment of remains, most likely of bovid and smaller size mammalian such as ovicaprical.	none					
211	Oik. Zafeiropoulou π1				Cremated	C	18 dry faunal fragments (2 innominate fragments [both of which showed the acetabulum] and 3 flat bone fragments, long/short tubular bone fragments, and one horn-cone fragment of an ovicaprical individual)	(R. parietal)	none	Male	YA	None due to limited preservation	None due to limited preservation	13.00
212	Oik. Zafeiropoulou, 28/8/1987, O1, bones of pipeline 1						dry faunal bone fragments included an assortment of dry bones representing Sus, ovicaprical sized, and smaller sized fauna.	none					

Key:
- equals Geometric Period Dry Single Individual Burial Context
- equals Geometric Period Cremated Single Individual Burial Context
- equals Geometric Period Faunal Remains
- equals Geometric Period Multiple Individual (some involving dry and cremated human individuals) Burial Contexts

TABLE 2

Categories	Single Interments		Multiple Interments		Count
Biological Assessment	Dry Form	Cremated Form	Dry Form	Cremated Form	
"Males"	1	19	1	5	26
"Probable Males"	1	1	1		3
"Possible Males"	1		1		2
"Females"	10		1		11
"Probable Females"	2				2
"Possible Females"	1				1
"Indeterminate"	6	1	3		10
Subtotals	22	21	7	5	55

TABLE 3

Age Subcategories Used in Age Assessing the Population Sample	Abbreviations	Age Range in Years
Infancy I	IN I	Birth-6
Infancy II	IN II	6.01*-12
Subadults	SA	12.01-<18
Subadults to Young Adults	SAYA	12.01-25
Young Adults	YA	18-25
Young Adults to Middle Adults	YAMA	18-35
Middle Adults	MA	25.01-35
Middle Adults to Late Adults	MALA	25-45
Late Adults	LA	35.01-45
General Adults	GA	18-45
Late Adults to Maturus	LAM	35-55
Senilis (Older)	S	55.01-65+
(*) : The decimal subdivision indicates that an age assessment rubric is considered between age subgroups		

TABLE 4

Basic Categories of Age Subgroups	Age Range in Years
Infancy I	Birth - 6
Infancy II	6.01* - 12
Subadult	12.01 - <18
Young Adult	18.01 - 25
Middle Adult	25.01 - 35
Late Adult	35.01 - 45
Maturus	45.01 - 55
Older (Senilis)	55.01 - 65+
(*) : The decimal subdivision indicates that an age assessment rubric is considered between age subgroups	

TABLE 5

\multicolumn{5}{	l	}{Variability of Bone Weight and Preservation among Cremation Contexts}
No. Contexts	Lab No.	Bone Weights in gr	Bone Weights in Ascending Scale	Valuations
1	5	730	13	
2	7	64	13	
3	8	187	13	
4	9	13	14	
5	10	188	34	
6	11	822	45	
7	12	285	47	
8	13	428	64	
9	16	149	66	
10	19	479	94	
11	21	94	149	
12	22	47	174	
13	23	301	187	
14	26a	45	188	
15	27	654	285	
16	29	34	301	
17	32	174	380	
18	33	66	428	
19	40	486	479	
20	36	13	486	
21	54	1337	654	
22	56	14	730	
23	129	816	816	
24	145	380	822	
25	147	963	963	
26	211	13	1337	
			8782	Sum
			13	Min
			1337	Max
			337.769	Average